FSC
www.fsc.org
MIX
Papier aus verantwortungsvollen Quellen
Paper from responsible sources
FSC® C105338

CHRIS A. YOUNG

M.E.

- How death row saved my life -

Dear reader,

I, as the publisher, may or may not agree with the content of this book, or parts of it, but it is and remains the unadulterated words of the author himself, edited as little as possible. I believe in freedom of speech and that the death penalty is wrong without any exception. There is a saying, "*You can tell the value of a society by how it treats the weakest of its members.*" I believe that to be true. That's why I give these members of society the opportunity to raise their voice. Most of them have undergone a transformation for the better. They have developed a mental strength in prison that we can't even imagine due to being locked up and forgotten about. Even after all these years they are still there; living, learning and rising beyond themselves. We can learn from them as much as they can learn from us. To silence one of them would be to silence all of us.

Stefan Heikens

Cover Design and Artwork: Stefan Heikens
Edited by: Nicole Niehoff / Stefan Heikens
Herstellung und Verlag: BoD – Books on Demand, Norderstedt
ISBN: 9783734794292

DEDICATION

I DEDICATE THIS BOOK TO MY GRANDMOTHER CHERYL, MY BEST FRIEND SONDRA AND MY BABY GIRL CHRISHELLE. THE THREE OF YOU HAVE POURED SO MUCH LOVE INTO ME.

GRANDMA, YOU ARE MY ROCK. THERE ARE NO WORDS TO EXPRESS HOW MUCH I LOVE YOU AND APPRECIATE ALL YOU HAVE DONE FOR ME. YOU KNOW HOW TO MAKE ME LAUGH AND MAKE ME CRY.

SONDRA, YOU ARE MY VERY BEST FRIEND. THANK YOU FOR YOUR LOVE, YOUR SUPPORT, YOUR VISITS, AND ALL THE WORK YOU HAVE PUT IN TO HELP ME WITH MY PROJECT TO REACH THESE KIDS. YOU ARE MY RIDE OR DIE GIRL. YOU HAVE SHOWN ME WHAT REAL TRUE FRIENDSHIP IS.

CHRISHELLE, YOU ARE MY BABY, MY PRINCESS AND YOU HOLD THE REINS TO YOUR DADDY'S HEART. YOU LIGHT UP MY WORLD, GIRL. I WANT YOU TO HAVE THE BEST LIFE HAS TO OFFER. YOU ARE BEAUTIFUL AND I AM SO LUCKY AND BLESSED THAT YOU ARE A PART OF ME. I WILL LOVE YOU FOREVER AND DON'T EVER FORGET IT. YOU BRING SUNSHINE INTO MY LIFE. DADDY LOVES YOU.

SPECIAL DEDICATION: LAURENCE, THANK YOU, MAN FOR EVERYTHING. I LOVE YOU, BRO.

CHRIS

FOREWORD
by Valerie Harris
Page 9

M.E. – MY EXPERIENCE
Page 13

LAST RIDE – LAST WORDS
Page 119

EPILOGUE
by Stefan Heikens
Page 125

FEBRUARY 17, 2019
by Valerie Harris
Page 133

CHRISTOPHER YOUNG
by Perry E. Williams
Page 137

FOREWORD BY VALERIE HARRIS

In the year 2004, I walked through the doors of Polunsky alongside my daughter Sondra for the very first time. Polunsky is a prison located in Livingston, TX. We were there to visit my nephew, Christopher Young. This would be the first time I would meet him as an adult because the last time I saw him, he was sitting on the steps of his home, after the funeral we attended of his best friend, his dad – my nephew. Chris did not attend the funeral. He was close to his dad. He waited for him to come home, and he never did. He was the tender age of 8 years old. Within the pages of this book, you will read the story of the life of Christopher Young and how he ended up on death row at Polunsky. When we sat down for the first time to visit him and our eyes met, I saw a boy. Through the years, as Sondra and I would visit him, I watched him grow into a man – a man with a vision. He had found his purpose. He had found a reason to fight to live. An artist, a scholar, a father, a nephew, a brother, a son, a friend, a mentor, a writer, a man who was locked up behind the prison walls who poured his life into a dream. This desire of his was to reach beyond the prison to effect change in the community in which he grew up. He learned that a life within this prison was not a place for young boys or troubled youth to come and live out their days. You will find within these pages how he rallied his prison brothers together to reach beyond the prison walls to effect change in the lives of troubled youths. He wanted to convince them that there was a better way and to motivate them to live, to grow, to heal, to thrive, to better themselves through education and non-violence, and to let them know that they were not alone. There were people who would listen, hear them, and help them through their inner struggles so they could become productive citizens instead of destructive, broken men and women. As you read this book, please listen to Chris' heart. Listen to his story before you judge the man. His life here on earth is gone, but his vision lives on. What was important to him was young people, so he planted the seed of change through what he called "*Reaching Our Young from the Inside Out*". It has now grown to a legacy for youth as it is being formulated as a Foundation for young people called "Love, Forgiveness, and Second Chances". The love of people, the love of life, the love of his children will never die. His love lives on. The vision lives on in the hearts of those who are still behind the prison walls who are working to fulfill the vision. Obie Weathers III, Tony Egbuna Ford, Tomas Gallo, Howard Guidry, James Broadnax, and Perry Williams have picked up the torch to reach and work beyond the prison walls to change young lives and to help heal the brokenness of a community. Love is the key. Forgiveness is the door. Second Chances is our hope and goal for a troubled generation of young lives. Reaching our Young from the Inside Out.

Valerie Harris

M.E. - MY EXPERIENCE

CHAPTER 1

2011: I am sitting in a concrete cell, stranded on Texas death row, waiting to be murdered by the state. I was convicted of murdering a convenience store clerk while attempting to rob him, if you let the state tell it. But none of that matters now. I am here, captured by four walls that have defeated some of the strongest men. The fight is not only for my life but for the preservation of my sanity. Sitting on a steel makeshift bed, I look in retrospect at the long journey that has brought me to this situation.

I was born on September 24, 1983 to Dannetta Brown and Willard Floyd "Chuck" Young in San Antonio, TX. Mom was only 17 years old when she delivered me into this world. She already had another child, my older sister Tasha, who was 3 years old. Dad was 21 years old and he already had another son, my older brother Donta, who was 2. Mom and dad conceived and delivered one more child together before they split. She is my younger sister Charlotte.

When I was 5 my mom packed us up and moved us to Milwaukee, Wisconsin. Mama has a couple of sisters that stayed there and she wanted to get her life on track. Mama met a new man named Clarence, who would play a significant role later in my life. Mama married Clarence and they produced my little brother Tyrone.

Because I was really young, a lot of my memories of that time are a blur. There is one experience that stood out to me, though. While living in Milwaukee, one day my aunt sent me, both of my sisters, my little brother and her daughter to the store. She had given us one quarter each. My aunt is a beautiful woman inside and out. She was the type of person that would do anything for her kids, nieces, and nephews. Her only problem, or so I thought, was she was a strict disciplinarian. She would whoop our ass for anything and she did not play when it came to an ass whooping! Whether with a belt, switch, extension cord, paddle, or her hand, you knew that ass whooping was going to hurt. As we were walking to the store, I was holding Tyrone's hand and his quarter. I was around 7 at the time and Tyrone was about 2. We all walked in the store and went our separate ways towards the goodies we wanted. I ran straight towards the ice cream freezer. I love ice cream. I looked around the freezer, rummaging through the different varieties and found a Nestle Crunch bar. I had to have that Nestle Crunch bar. It was calling my name. I had one problem. It was fifty cents. I was 7 and I was just learning how to add. I knew that my quarter and Tyrone's quarter would equal fifty cents. I grabbed the ice cream, even though I did not have enough money, but I had the intention of sharing the ice cream with my brother for the price of his quarter. I looked at Tyrone; showing him the ice cream bar, waving it in the air.

"Tyrrrooonee, do you want to share this with me?" He eyed it, eyes bulging out. "Yes, I will share it with you."

We went to the counter to pay for the ice cream bar. The clerk said, “That will be fifty cent.”

I placed my quarter on the counter and then gave Tyrone his quarter to place on the counter so we could both pay for the ice cream. We paid for the ice cream and walked out the store waiting on the rest of the bunch to finish with their purchases. Once outside we started to eat the ice cream. When my sisters and cousin came out of the store they asked, “What did Tyrone get?”

“He got this,” I was holding up the bar for them to see.

I don’t know if they heard what I said but they did not ask any more questions. We walked home. When we arrived home my aunt asked, “Where is Tyrone’s stuff? What did he get?”

Tyrone always was her favorite. I told her, with ice cream around my mouth and hands all sticky, “We shared this ice cream.”

I could tell by her body language that she was pissed. There was no way she could have thought I was lying because Tyrone’s face and hands were sticky too. Aunt Janet told me to take my black ass outside to get a switch. Like most kids, I went to find the smallest switch on the tree. I broke the switch off the branch, cleaned the leaves, and brought it in the house to Aunt Janet. I thought the whooping was not going to hurt as bad since I did get the smallest switch.

When Aunt Janet saw the twig I brought in to her, she snatched it, popped me with it, and said,

"Go get another switch and it better be longer than this."

I went back outside and picked another one. I remember thinking, "I'm picking a switch to get my ass whooped behind a damn quarter." When I brought the switch back she whipped my ass. Aunt Janet gave us the worst whooping. She didn't just whoop us and let us go on our way. She made us understand what we did wrong and what we were getting a whooping for. Or at least she thought she did.

When she finished, she had me facing the wall with one leg bent at the knee. She said every time that my leg hit the ground I would get another ass whooping. I don't know how long I stood there but I don't remember my leg hitting the ground either. All this behind a damn quarter! To this day, I still love my Aunt Janet dearly and still talk to her occasionally. I still don't understand why I got that whooping that day.

This was one of the early stages of someone trying to set me straight. Maybe she saw something that day that would affect me in the future. I have never asked her about it since.

CHAPTER 2

After living in Milwaukee a few years, my mom moved us back to San Antonio. I was in the second grade and we lived on a street with exactly four houses on it. Across the street was a *Mrs. Baird's bakery*. Every morning we would wake up to the smell of fresh bread. My mom would send us to the bakery to pick up milk and bread occasionally. Because the store workers knew us, we'd leave with bags of "day old" pastries, bread and rolls. Sometimes when we were outside playing with the other kids we would sneak off to the bakery knowing they would send us off with plenty of goodies.

Before we left Milwaukee my mom married Clarence, Tyrone's father. Clarence was real cool. I cannot remember Clarence ever giving us any whooping, but if he did, it wasn't anything serious because I have had some horrible whoopings! Clarence was a big kid who liked to sit in front of the Nintendo and play *Super Mario Brothers* for hours. Sometimes he would even let us play with him, but most of the time we would just sit and watch. My dad would come by and pick us up all the time. He would either take us to my grandmother's or my great-grandparents' house. My great-grandmother, "Nan-Nan," was a saint! She used to spoil us crazy. When we went to her house we would all sit with her and play Keno for pennies. She always put dollars to our pennies and we played for hours. After letting us win the money she was going to give us anyway, we would sit and watch television and/or crochet. My great-grandfather, "Granddaddy," really was a character. He was a World War II vet. After being discharged from the military he became a chef on the *Southern Pacific Railroad*. He did this for forty years. This man could cook. He loved cooking so much that if he asked if you were hungry and you told him no, he would curse you out. I mean he did not care who you were or how old you were. He would curse you out as if you stole something from him. After he finally calmed down and stopped cursing for about ten minutes, he'd ask if you were hungry again, as if you didn't say no the first time. This might have been a part of his *Post Traumatic Stress Disorder* (PTSD) from the war and the cooking probably was therapy to him. This time when you answered you already knew the consequences of saying no, so the best thing to say was yes and let him do his thing. This started a whole round of other questions. He asked what you wanted to eat and you had better think of something or suffer his next flurry of verbal blows again. The best thing about his meals was that he spared not one ingredient in his recipes. If he made you some gumbo you would have the whole sea in the pot and it was all finger-licking good. Plus, you would lick the bowl without a care in the world even if someone was watching.

The only person he would bow down to was Nan-Nan. My Nan-Nan was in some type of accident in her younger days that left her paralyzed from the waist down and confined her to bed. This took nothing from her but her ability to walk. I've seen this woman conduct business from that bed that will make any corporate CEO of a Fortune 500 company envious. I remember when my Nan-Nan and Granddaddy used to argue. Usually Granddaddy would get tipsy from the *Schaeffer's beer* that they used to drink and say something to us about running around the house. Once Nan-Nan would hear that she would say something to him and they would start cursing at each other. Granddaddy never won! We'd sit in the room with her while she would go off on him and we would laugh. She laughed right along with us. Eventually, Granddaddy would shut up. They were a lovely couple. Looking back on them, I know that my Granddaddy loved her dearly. I wish I would have learned love on that level when I was in the world.

A few months after I turned eight, it was Martin Luther King's birthday. The *Martin Luther King* march in San Antonio was the largest march in America. It was a major event in San Antonio. Later in life, I would spend most of the year getting ready for the march, painting my car and making sure I had rims on it like other individuals would. My dad planned to pick us up early and take us to Nan-Nan and Granddaddy's house because the march would pass in front of their home. He watched the march and then dad would take us where the march ended and the festivals began. The first part of the day went as planned. Dad came and picked us up and we watched the march pass in front of our great-grandparents' yard. Then my dad took us home and said he would be right back to pick us up to head to where the march ended and the festivals began. I protested. I wanted to go everywhere with my father. Usually, he would take me. This day, he said he would be right back. Dad never came back to pick us up. I was pissed. I wasn't mad that I missed the Martin Luther King festivities. I was mad because I felt like my dad lied to me, something he never did.

We waited all day for him to come back for us. He never returned. When night fell, the police showed up at our house. They talked to my mom for a moment and I saw her break down crying. At that time, I still did not know what was going on. When the police left, my mom sat me down and told me what happened. I don't remember if I cried or not, but I do know a huge part of me died that day. The next day, mama told me I did not have to go to school. I went anyway. I refused to sit around all day and do nothing. That would have left me too much time to think about my dad. School was the closet I went to hide in. On the day of my dad's wake I saw his body for the last time. I remember walking inside the funeral home up to the casket. I seen him laying there made up from the make-up the mortician caked on him. I turned around and walked out of the funeral home. I sat on the steps for the rest of the procession. I couldn't see my father like that. It was too much of a realization that he was dead. I think I wanted myself to believe that he was still alive. The next day was his funeral. I went to school instead. A few months later, my mom found out that my sister Tasha was pregnant.

My sister was only 12 years old, so I could only imagine what was going through my mother's head at the time. I would think that she was furious, that is, until my sister dropped a bomb on her. Clarence, my mom's husband, had been raping my sister and had impregnated her. I was too young to understand at the time but I remember us moving again, and Clarence going to jail. It seemed like life was going downhill. Too much was happening at one time. When my dad was murdered, I didn't talk to anyone. I would bottle up my feelings and walk around like his death didn't bother me. Everybody could see it in my face, but in my mind I was hiding it.

I spent weeks at a time at my Aunt Velina's house. She had four children at the time and I enjoyed being around family. I remember I would wake up in the middle of the night screaming out for my daddy. All of the emotions I was repressing would manifest themselves in my dreams and hunt me like the fictional character Freddie Kruger did to his victims.

There was this videotape that I used to watch. It was the reenactment of my dad's murder that the news station played on the night of his death. The tape showed four actors in the car arguing. The actor directly behind the driver pulled out a gun and shot the driver in the back of the head, blowing his brains all over the windshield. Then, the actors pulled the driver out of the car and laid him on the side of the street. They drove off in the driver's car. The driver was supposed to be my father. I watched that tape so many times that to this day I still remember every detail, every sound and every voice as vividly as if I watched it yesterday.

Aunt Velina lived in the projects called *Olive Park East* located on the east side of San Antonio. The projects were full of kids and everyone knew each other. We were like one huge family. These projects were also gang infested and gang controlled. It was a well-known Blood neighborhood. The *Blood Stone Villains* controlled Olive Park and its sister projects located directly behind them called Village East. I lived over there.

The other place I enjoyed to escape to was my great-grandparents' house. My dad used to live with them and they were really close to him. My great-grandparents treated me and my siblings as if we were their children. Nan-Nan was heartbroken when my father was murdered. Granddaddy was also, but like me, he kept his feelings bottled inside.

She died not too long after my father did. I cannot remember the reason for her passing, but I think it was old age and a broken heart. Granddaddy didn't last long either. After Nan-Nan died, I watched Granddaddy rapidly deteriorate. He couldn't function without his wife. He died months after she did. I knew he died of a broken heart. Nan-Nan was his world and although she was confined to a bed, she ran the household.

After their deaths I felt lost. Everyone I loved was dying back to back. I felt I didn't have anywhere to go or anyone to turn to. Of course, I still went to my aunt's house but it felt different. I felt I had a huge hole in my heart that was widening from all the loss. I did not understand death at the time, so these experiences were new to me and I didn't know how to deal with them.

My mom and I never had a close relationship. There were times I wanted to talk to her, but I couldn't. She was just a kid herself and I think she was dealing with the deaths in her own way. I can't even say she would have told me anything helpful back then anyway. The only thing I knew to do was to go to school where there was something for me to do and keep my mind occupied. This brought along a whole new beast.

Before Nan-Nan passed away she bought me a violin. She encouraged me to play for the school orchestra. In passing I may have told her I was interested or something along those lines. She listened and purchased me a violin. This was major in my school. I went to *Dorie Miller Elementary* at the time and was about 8 years old. Dorie Miller was located on the east side of San Antonio, a part of town that is highly impoverished, drug, and gang infested. The majority of the kids who went to this school, me included, were from single parent homes that were barely making ends meet. When I showed up to school with the violin, I was the talk of the playground. I was always looked at as the nerd, and now, that was confirmed with the violin. Not only was I a confirmed nerd, now it appeared I had money. I did not care at the time. I just loved school and enjoyed being there. I suffered a lot of ridicule from the other kids. When I showed up to practice with my own violin, the teacher accepted me in the band on the spot. I learned how to play the violin, viola, bass and the cello. At the same time I played in the school's orchestra, I was in the school's chess club too. I was the captain of the team and have participated in numerous chess tournaments.

It wasn't too soon that the news spread around school that my father was murdered. Kids around the school would bring that up whenever I would get into an argument with them. They would say: "That's why you don't have a daddy", "That's why your daddy is dead", etc. I've heard them all.

One day I snapped. I was tired of being picked on. I was tired of being called a nerd. I was tired of being called a fatherless child. All of the anger, depression and stress that was built up in me came out. I went on a fighting spree. I would fight anyone that would even look at me crazy. If they even looked like they had something to say about me not having a father, I would fight them. After showing kids that I wouldn't put up with their ridicule anymore, they stopped.

Life was not all tragedy and sorrow back then. I used to love the house we lived in. It had six rooms, but it was small and cozy. The living room wasn't that big, but we had somewhere to call home. We had a kitchen, bathroom, and three bedrooms, two in which my brothers and sisters shared. The house was located on a dead end street that ended at an entrance ramp of the expressway that ran right along the side. We went to sleep listening to cars on the freeway fly by and eighteen wheelers rumble past. The streets were filled with kids to play with, plus we were allowed to go to the street behind us. Between 1991 and 1992, I remember I had been shot for the first time by a BB gun.

I had a friend who lived down the street, and his dad had all types of guns, real and fake. We knew we couldn't mess with the real guns so we would play with the fake guns, the BB and pellet guns. We used to have these wars, something similar to Cowboys and Indians, but ours were called Bloods and Crips. *Gangbanging* was very popular in the 90's in San Antonio. Most of the members from California moved to Texas and brought the culture with them. Everybody who was young and looking for an outlet against the hardships gravitated to gangs. When we played Bloods and Crips we shot real BBs and real pellets, and we would oftentimes load our guns with arrowhead pellets.

I remember the moment I was hit with a BB. I think I was the only one ever hit with a BB or pellet. We didn't know how to aim and shoot. That was never taught on television. All we knew was to pull the trigger. I was hit in the arm. It felt like a bee sting, but the thing about that was I hated bees. So when I was hit I thought I was stung by a bee and thought I was going to die. Not only was I scared of dying, I was scared to tell my mom in fear of getting my ass whooped for playing with guns. We patched it up and passed it off as some type of wound that happens to young kids when they play. In the neighborhood where we lived, crime was prevalent. Although we knew crime was occurring in the area, we paid it no mind until crime hit close to home again.

There were a lot of mysteries surrounding my mom. She partied all night at the clubs and had men at our house all of the time. We didn't care what was going on as long as we got half of what we asked for. She would send us to the store with a book of food stamps each. Yes, she would take the big bills out and leave the ones and fives. But to a child, that was a lot of money.

One day, my siblings and I were getting dressed for school. It was early in the morning, and I was in my room getting Tyrone and me dressed when I saw a shadow go across my window. I didn't pay it too much mind until I heard the front door get kicked in. I heard the police yelling, "GET DOWN! GET DOWN! POLICE! POLICE!"

I didn't move. I stood there with Tyrone and watched what was unfolding in front of our eyes. I witnessed the police cuff my mom and take her to jail. She had her current boyfriend there at the time so the police did not remove us from our home. I was in shock. All I knew was that the police had taken my mom to jail and we didn't know when she was coming back.

We went to school like any other day, but I did not function the same like I usually did at school. I couldn't think with my mom being in jail. I didn't think she did anything wrong so I was mad at the police for taking her there. When I returned home from school and my mom still was not home, I began to panic. I didn't know what we were going to do. My aunt came to the house and took care of us. We went to school the next day as usual and caught word that our mom went to jail. We didn't hear the usual ridicule that one would receive. In fact, we received praise. Our mom had passed the "hood test" and was a certified "hood" mom since she went to jail. Nobody knew why she went to jail but none of that mattered. Not too many moms in the hood went to jail, so that gave me a sort of hood status.

While all this was going on, I was still going to my Aunt Velina's house in Olive Park. It was normal to see numerous gang members at her house. They would be drinking 40 oz of *Olde English 800* malt liquor and smoking cigarettes. I don't remember if they were smoking marijuana at the time. I used to watch the way they interacted with one another; the laughs, the slaps on the back, and the sparring they did. It signified love in my eyes. With the guys being like uncles to me I knew I wanted to be like them, so I asked what did it take to become a Blood? They laughed at me telling me that I was too young. I was 8 at the time and I felt I didn't have the love surrounding me. I knew that I would do what I had to do to be like them no matter how old I was.

The first few times I asked, they continued to ignore me. I would do foolish things just to show them that I was one of them. Things that would mimic them, such as wearing all red whenever I went to my Aunt's house (even two or three different reds that didn't match), move like they moved, talk like they talked, etc.

Then one day, my Uncle Michael showed me something that made me make my decision on really wanting to be a member. It was one of those overcast days outside. One of those days where the clouds would pass by and drop a few minutes of rain. Just enough rain to disrupt a good basketball game. We were standing in the breezeway of the apartment building waiting on another cloud to pass by when I noticed a big patch on Michael's arm. I asked him what had happened to him. He looked at me and said, "I got popped."

Me not knowing what the full hood lingo meant, instead of asking him what "popped" meant, I asked him to let me see the scar. He peeled off the patch and showed me the hole in his arm and the bruise around it. He told me that the Crips caught him "slipping" (out of his territory) and popped him, hitting him in the arm. From that point on I knew that I wanted to be a Blood, and that I didn't like Crips.

A few visits later, me and my older brother Donta were in the courtyard talking with some other friends when my uncle and some of his friends approached us. They told us they were going to put us down, meaning they were going to initiate us in the gang family. We looked at them dumbfounded and probably a bit scared not knowing what was going to happen. They started to beat us up. They didn't hold back anything, and told us that if we ran and didn't fight, we would not be able to be in the gang. We fought harder than we ever did before because none of us wanted to look bad in front of one another. The beating went on for almost five minutes. Then they all stopped with us laying on the ground hurt, but none of us ran and all of us fought back. They had a sense of pride while looking at us. They told us to recite the oath and repeat after them, "*Blood in, Blood out.*" We did and became members of the *Blood Stone Villains*.

We started to do our own thing around the neighborhood. We were involved in all kinds of mischief. We started to venture further than we were allowed around the neighborhood, staying out past the time the streetlights came on, and rebelling a lot more. My mom saw the change in my ways and stopped letting me go to my Aunt's house while she lived in Olive Park. It was too late. I was in and I wasn't stopping. The neighborhood we lived in was predominantly Crips. I started getting into a lot more fights with the kids that were initiated like I was. At school my production didn't drop but my focus wasn't on school anymore. My focus was on gangbanging. I was only in the fourth grade.

When I went to the sixth grade I was excited. I got to go to a new school, a middle school. It was a school that everybody talked about because of the gang activity that went on there. The name of the school was *Martin Luther King Middle School*. How ironic! The school was located in a Blood neighborhood called the Stixx. The kids from other neighborhoods had to attend *MLK middle school* because of the school zone they fell under. This made for a powder keg for all children looking for validation in the hood from the Elders, the O.G.s.

We would stand around the playground in two groups. One group dressed in all red and the other group dressed in all blue. Nothing major happened but a bunch of stare downs and the occasional fight, but the tension was as thick as a sirloin steak. In the first six months I was constantly getting into confrontations with the teachers. I was sent to a new class the school created for "problem" kids. Once I got into that class, I knew I was going to have a problem there. The class was a mixture of gang members that had been told that they were "bad!" What else does a kid that is already looking for validation in the streets need than for the school to tell them they are bad and have to be placed in a special class because of their behavior?

I walked in the class, took my seat, and was handed the work the teacher had for me. While I was working, this kid got up, walked past my desk, and took a pencil I had laying there. I looked at him and laughed. I knew a test when I saw one and this was a test since I was new to the class. The teacher didn't see him grab the pencil though. I said to him, "Put my shit back!"

He laughed at me and walked to the pencil sharpener and sharpened my pencil. While he was coming back towards me, I got out of my seat and punched him straight in the face. He was not expecting it so he grabbed his nose. I kept punching him until the teacher broke us up and told him to go back to his seat. She told me to step outside the classroom. I went back to my desk, ignoring her instead. I knew she thought I had started the fight since all she saw was me get up and hit him.

When I was back in my seat she told me again to go outside the classroom. I blew up, knowing I was being punished for starting the fight. When I got out of my desk, I pushed the desk back and it tipped over on her toe. I didn't know it happened because I was already headed for the door. I stepped into the hallway and waited for her to come out.

I waited for about thirty minutes when two San Antonio police officers came walking down the hall towards me. They placed me in handcuffs, took me to the principal's office, and told the principal they were taking me to jail. I thought I was going to jail for the fight so I told the officer that I didn't start the fight and asked why I had to go to jail. I told the officer that the other guy walked up to me and took my pencil. They didn't pay me any attention and just led me to the police car. While we were riding to the detention center one of the officers said, "So, you like to beat up teachers?"

I looked at him crazy and lost at the same time and asked, "What are you talking about? I had a fight with this other kid like I had been trying to tell you."

He replied, “That’s not what we heard. We heard you picked up the desk and threw it at her, breaking her toe.”

“I didn’t throw a desk at her. All I had was a fight,” I said.

The police officers stopped talking to me. We pulled up to the detention center and they took me inside. The first thing I was asked was if I was a gang member.

Now, this question has numerous implications. I immediately thought that gang members were treated worse and that’s not what I wanted so I told them “No.” They stripped me out and put me through my first full body strip search, showered me, and gave me a change of clothes, which were a size too big for me. By the time I was housed, it was night time and the mod (housing unit) I was placed in was already locked up for the night. The next morning we were let out of our cells and I seen a mod full of Crips.

When they saw me they knew something was wrong because I didn’t belong there. I knew at that moment I was going to have to fight. Instead of me fighting, they asked me what happened for me to get there. I told them about the fight I had and about what the teacher said I did. They asked me how I ended up in their mod. I told them I didn’t know. They asked what I told the intake officer when he asked if I was a gang member. I told them that I said that I wasn’t a gang member. They told me that was the reason why I was in their mod. What the officer did was look up my address and saw I lived in a Crip neighborhood so he put me around the Crips. I was lucky I knew the kids that were in there.

That same day I was released in the custody of my mother. I never went back to *MLK middle school* again. I was 11 years old and that was the first time I went to jail, but definitely not my last.

CHAPTER 3

My mom was waiting on *section 8 government housing* when a house became available for us. What the government housing agency did was move all the qualified Eastside families to the suburbs on the nice side of town. We moved into our new home. The house was two stories high and consisted of three bedrooms and two bathrooms. We also had a one car garage. We thought we were rich. We felt like the Beverly Hillbillies when they moved to Beverly Hills. With the move, I had to change schools again. The new school I went to was called *Woodlake Elementary*. I was the only person I knew that went from a Middle School back to an Elementary School. *Woodlake*'s grading system did not end at the fifth grade like the Elementary on the Eastside did. *Woodlake* ended with the sixth grade. When I got there I immediately knew I was more mature than all the other six graders there. I was the only real gang member there and I was looked up to because I was from the "ghetto," the Eastside. I was only 11 and had been taking gang banging seriously since before I left *MLK Middle School*. *Woodlake* did no favors for my ego at that time. I loved the attention I was getting from my classmates.

At *Woodlake* they let us take our walkman to school, something they never let us do on the Eastside. One day I brought my cassette player with the tape Dr. Dre's *The Chronic*. At that time, *The Chronic* was the album in the hood that everybody was listening to. It was an album that spoke of the gangsta lifestyle we were living, and the lifestyle the kids at *Woodlake* dreamed of. When everyone found out what I was listening to, they all wanted to hear it. They told me that their parents would not allow them to listen to anything like that. I passed it around and let everyone listen to it. The teacher saw the interest and wanted to know what we were listening to. Once she heard the lyrics by Dr. Dre she took the tape from me and sent me to the principal's office. They called my mom to let her know what I had been listening to at school and that it was unacceptable. They sent me home with a note and the tape for my mom to sign to let them know that she received the tape. When I got home my mom was pissed. She wasn't mad at me for listening to Dr. Dre or taking the tape to school. She was mad at me for almost losing her tape. I got an ass whooping for that.

For the seventh grade I had to change schools once again. I was headed back to middle school or junior high, as the rich side of town called it. I went to *Kirby Jr. High School* in Kirby, Texas. This school was like a different world for me. The gang mentality was not popular there. It was all about stylish clothes and how much money one came to school with. These were two races that I knew I wasn't going to win. So I did the next best thing to win the popularity contest, I played sports. I joined the football team.

When I joined the team, I was a long way from making it. They didn't know where to put me.

I wanted to play quarterback, but when I tried out, I had no arm strength and couldn't get the ball to the receiver, even if the receiver grabbed it out of my hand. Because of that, I made the second team. *Kirby* had two teams for both grades (7th and 8th): a blue team (the first team) and a white team (the second team). The white team played the second team from the other schools.

When I played my first game, the coach wouldn't call any pass plays, knowing I couldn't throw the football. We were up in the fourth quarter so he tried one. I knew the play and probably could have executed it, but my main problem wasn't throwing the ball. My main problem was I was afraid of getting hit! I didn't want to stand back there and take a shot. This was a blessing and a curse. The curse was there was no passing diversity to our attack. When he called the play, I took off running. The first time I ran for about 80+ yards and got caught before I scored. The second time he called the play, I took off again running for 70+ yards but this time scoring. He found his blessing. Every game we played I would run for a touchdown untouched.

When I went into my 8th grade year, I was asked to start as quarterback for the blue team. I refused out of rebellion and being that most of my friends were on the white team. That 8th grade year, I did the same thing. I ran for touchdown after touchdown. Before I went to the 9th grade high school, I was asked by coaches to play football when I got to high school, but they suggested I play running back. I told them I would think about it. I went to the 9th grade at *Judson High School* in Converse, TX.

Judson is known as the top team in the state of Texas when it comes to high school football, which is a huge sport in the state. *Judson High School* was a large school. It was the only high school in the district being fed students from over fifteen middle and junior high schools. The campus was split in two, one for the 9th and 10th graders called The Gray Campus, and the other was for the 11th and 12th graders called the Red Campus. This school had its own football stadium that would rival most professional sport teams.

When I first arrived there it was the first school that I went to that gave the students a bunch of freedom. I was 13 years old at the time. The school made the students responsible for getting to class without monitoring the hallways, going to lunch, buying their food and getting home by themselves. I've never had that in my life. Every school I went to watched us like a hawk. I didn't like the students or the teachers there. Most of the students were jocks with rich families or real preppy students that would turn their noses up at people like me. *Judson* was the first place I experienced racism.

When I went to school I had my own style of dress that was labeled as "gang attire." It mostly consisted of Dickie pants (workmen pants) and a long T-shirt with matching Converse shoes. All my clothes were red. The entire outfit may have cost

$30.00 which was cheap compared to the $100 Jordan tennis shoes most of the kids were wearing. My mom couldn't afford Jordans, and besides, Jordans weren't my style anyway.

One day I saw this white girl that I wanted to talk to. This was a big step for me because I didn't like white women because of my past experience with one. I walked up to her and asked her name.

"What's your name?" I asked, smiling.

She looked at me, turned her head with this frown of scorn on her face, turned her nose up, turned to her friends and said, "Look at this gang-banging Nigger!"

They all laughed and walked away. I wasn't shocked. It just reinforced the feelings I had for white women. I knew they weren't racist because white women talked to Blacks all the time. I was just stereotyped for the way I dressed and me being a known gang member. I guess niggers are the only gang members.

Around this time, I was growing up and becoming very rebellious. One day, my mother and I got into an argument. I don't remember what it was about, but it had to be bad. She whooped the shit out of me with a belt. I was immune to the whooping by now and a belt did nothing to me. When she swung the first time and struck me, I just stood there without any reaction. She struck me again, and still, I had no reaction. She dropped the belt and started to punch me, yelling that I am not too big to get my ass kicked. I stood there and took it. When I got tired, I just walked off, passing by her, trying to make it out the door. She pulled out her stun gun and tried to tase me with it. I ran down the stairs of the house and went out the door. She didn't follow me.

I sat on the porch and after about ten minutes, the police showed up and put me in cuffs. She came outside once the cop showed up and told them to take me to jail because I had hit her. I pleaded with the officer, thinking he would listen, telling him that I didn't hit her. It fell on deaf ears. Here, I was headed back to jail. I was only 13 and this was my second trip. I went through the same process as the first time, but this time when the intake officer asked me if I was in a gang, I said yes, and that I was a Blood. He placed me in a mod full of Bloods.

When I went to juvenile detention the second time, I stayed there for almost three months. It was a simple assault, but since my mother did not want to get me out, I had to sit there. One day I went to court and I saw my grandmother there. My case was called and she stepped up saying she wanted me to be released into her custody. She stated she would have picked me up but she never knew that I was locked up. I was released, placed on probation and I moved into her house, back on the Eastside. It was the best move I made.

At my grandma's house there was a lot of love and very little rule. She told me: no smoking weed in the house, no girls in the house, and if I was going to be out late to call and let her know I was alright. Her biggest rule was that I had to go to work or go to school. Since I was only 13, I had to go to school.

I went to *Roosevelt High School*, even though *Roosevelt* was not in our district. I was zoned to *Sam Houston High School*, but *Sam Houston* was like a *Martin Luther King Middle School* on steroids. The gang activity there was so rampant that this school had metal detectors. My grandma knew if I went to that school that I was going to get in trouble. She knew about me being a gang member and she knew about the gang culture. She raised my Uncle Michael who is doing fifty years in prison now for murder, and she knew the signs, so she sent me to school across town. *Roosevelt High* was mixed with all types of personalities.

I liked going to that school because I didn't have anyone watching me over there. I didn't stay there long because I moved with my grandpa on the other side of town. I don't know what caused that move but I had to change schools again. I moved to *Robert E. Lee High School*. This school was pure racist. In the front of the school was a huge Confederate flag, which is a blatant symbol of slavery and racism. It was majority whites and the culture there was, for lack of better words to describe it, "redneck." The students wore tight jean pants, cowboy boots and cowboy hats. They drove big trucks to school with the Confederate flag waving on the back of the rack in the truck bed. They didn't associate with the blacks or Hispanics that were there and they used "nigger" and "spic" like they were telling you hello.

Racism never really bothered me on the surface. I didn't really understand the complex intricacies of racism, but I knew that the word nigger was a derogatory term for blacks and spic was one for Hispanics. I didn't talk to anybody but females. I was shunned for being a gang member and was shunned for being black. Females were the only ones that accepted me. That was fine with me because females were the only ones I wanted to be around in the first place.

Me and my grandpa didn't really get along. He didn't know how to raise any children. He didn't even raise his own, plus I didn't know him very well, so our communication wasn't as it should be. He owned a Jamaican BBQ Restaurant, and every day after school I had to ride the city bus straight to work. I would work at the restaurant until closing time and we would ride home together. This was our everyday routine. I don't think he ever left me in his house by myself. I knew he didn't trust me. In fact, he didn't trust anyone. I eventually got fed up with the living arrangement so I told him I didn't want to live there anymore. He was fine with that because I don't think he wanted me living there anyways. I ended up moving with my Aunt. After just a few months of living with my grandpa and going to *Lee High School*, I once again changed homes and school.

The district that my Aunt lived in was very upper-class suburban and about 90% whites during this time. I transferred to *Douglas MacArthur High School*. From the time I walked in the door, I didn't like the school. All of the teachers were white, as well as the majority of the students. I was not accepted and I never felt comfortable there. Although I was not looking for acceptance from anyone, I had to feel comfortable around people if I was going to interact with them. If I didn't feel comfortable around someone, I would completely shut down. I always did all of my work at all the schools I went to and my grades showed it, but I hated staying in the classroom when I was done with my work. I would just leave and find something to do.

I only stayed at *MacArthur High School* for a couple of months. The school year was coming to an end and it was still my first year in the 9th grade. I moved back in with my grandma over the summer, and because of that, the next year I went back to *Roosevelt High.* This time around, I didn't care. Here I was in the 9th grade for the second year, older than the rest of the kids in the class. I wouldn't stay in my class let alone stay in school the full day. After three to four months at *Roosevelt*, I was expelled.

My grandma wanted me to stay in school instead of getting a job, so I moved back with my mom and went back to *Judson High School.* This time when I enrolled there, the school sent me straight to their alternative school.

Although *Judson High* was a rich preppy school, their alternative school was structured like a small jail. They made each student wear bright yellow shirts with a number on the back. We were transported to and from school in a bus with bars on the windows and the campus had a strong police presence. I went there for a week and refused to go back.

My mom and I got into an argument about me not wanting to go back to school, so she kicked me out the house. I lived on the streets with friends around the neighborhood. I would break into houses during the day to support myself. Of course, that didn't last long. I got caught breaking into a house and was sent back to juvenile for the third time. I stayed there for a month and a half before my grandma came to get me out. She told me that I wasn't going to live with anyone else since I didn't get into trouble at her house.

When I moved back in with her, I found a job at a detail shop around the corner from the house. My uncle was married to the owner's mother and that's how I got the job there. I started working for Dollar Bills Auto Detail Shop at the age of 14 and kept that job until I was 21. It was off and on the entire time, but I always had a job at the detail shop if I needed it.

CHAPTER 4

My first experience with sex was not a good one. I was 5 years old and we were living in Milwaukee Wisconsin. My mom used to go to the nightclub and allowed our neighbor to babysit us. I can't remember how old she was, but I think she was around 13 or 14 at the time. She had a sister my age. Her sister was my best friend and we used to play every day. Whenever she would babysit us she would bring her sister Nicole with her. One day while I was at their house she told me and her sister to play a game. We played house and Nicole and I were married. She had us get naked and "showed" us what sex was. After she showed us what sex was, she asked me to give her oral sex. I didn't know the first thing about oral sex and neither did she, but I did it. She also gave me oral sex. Nicole and I thought the game we played was okay so one day we had nothing to do. We had sex. We were in the backyard of her house. There was a mattress back there, so we stripped naked like her sister showed us. We laid on the mattress and I got on top of her and started "having sex." There was no penetration. We were 5 and 6 at the time, but we did "it." As we were getting up my older sister Tasha was coming out of the house. She saw us naked and ran and got my mother, telling her that we were in the backyard naked. My mom came outside and whooped my ass all the way into the house. I was conflicted with emotions. I didn't know what I did wrong. I was taught that sex was a game and it was done for fun. I was scared to speak out on it because if I got a whooping once, I figured speaking out on it would get me another whooping. To this day, I never spoke about that incident. I never told my mom what happened. Instead of me telling anybody, I developed resentment for white women, thinking all white women were the same, and deceived men the way I was deceived. For years, I lived like that. Not until recently did I come to realize that she didn't do that to me because she was white. She did that to me because she was sick and someone taught her it was ok. I have met numerous white women that didn't act the same way. That time at *Judson HS* was my first attempt to try and talk to a white woman and even that attempt went sour.

As I grew up, sex was not very important to me. When I was 13, I finally lost my virginity to my next door neighbor who was 11 at the time. We had sex almost every day until one day we got caught. My mom beat the shit out of both of us and then her mom beat the shit out of both of us. We never stopped. We just tried to hide it better. Obviously, we didn't do a good job at it because we were caught numerous times after that. When I was at *Kirby Jr. HS*, I dated this girl named K. Young. She was just my type, tall and chocolate. We used to walk around school telling people we were married since we had the same last name.

One day she asked me to walk her home from school. Her house wasn't far from the school, but mine was a bus ride away. I told her I would walk her home, and I would just walk home afterwards. The first time I walked her home we stood on the side of the house and french kissed for about two hours. She wouldn't let me come inside because her mom was coming home any minute. When I walked home after coming from her house, it took me an hour which made me get home between 6:30 pm and 7:00 pm. School let out at 3:00 pm. I came home like this every day. My mom would ask me where I had been. I would tell her I stayed late for football practice and a few players walked home. She believed me for that whole football season.

Once the season was over the lie wouldn't work anymore, so I just told her the truth. I told her I had a girlfriend and I was walking her home from school every day. She put me on the most severe punishment that I've ever been on. I couldn't leave my room for anything but to use the restroom and eat dinner. My room was on the second floor and my window faced the backyard. My view was nothing but the back of people's homes. This went on for almost six months. Eventually, me and K broke up, and it was well before I got off punishment. Although I continued to walk her home, I never did have sex with her. This was my first experience with isolation housing.

I remember the first time I caught crabs. I was having sex with this girl who was straight out the ghetto. I was about 16 at the time and living with my grandma. I was at work one day and kept scratching my groin area. I didn't think anything of it. I went home early that day, and was in the restroom sitting on the toilet, picking through my groin hairs. I picked one of the bugs off of me and looked at it. I was shocked at what I was seeing. It looked like a small crab and it was moving! I threw it in the toilet, cleaned up, and went to tell my grandma.

"Grandma, I have some bugs on my stuff and it itches."

She asked to let her see.

I said, "Grandma, I am not letting you see my stuff!"

"Boy, I changed your diapers. I seen you before," she replied back.

I smiled and said, "Grandma, it is not the same as when I wore diapers."

She grabbed my belt, pulled me to her, and opened my pants. This may have been the most embarrassing moment in my life. Here I am standing in front of my grandma with my penis hanging out while she looked at an STD I contracted. She looked through my pubic hairs searching for the bugs.

She found one, pulled it off and said, "You've been fucking some nasty ass hoes! Go to the bathroom, shave all your hair off, and wash with this soap."

She handed me this black soap out of the cabinet. I was pissed. I wasn't mad that I had crabs, I was mad that I had to shave all my pubic hairs off. I just grew them and I was proud of them! There was no way I was cutting those. It took me sixteen years to get them. I did what my grandma said and the crabs went away. I did go back and have sex with the girl again. She must have cleaned herself also because I didn't catch it again.

CHAPTER 5

Life was hard during my years living with my grandmother. Not because there wasn't any love in her home but because there was too much love in her home. I had too much freedom to do what I wanted. I could engage in all the gang activity and drug dealing I wanted to. I started selling crack cocaine at the age of 14. I didn't have to because the detail shop was paying good money, but I did it because it was easy and available. Selling crack brought in a lot of money.

I bought my first car at the age of 15. It was a 1979 Cutlass Supreme. I was one of the few 15-year-olds with a car at the time. A few months later, I bought another car, a 1983 Fleetwood Cadillac. I now had two cars and more money than a 15-year-old could handle. My grandma knew what I was doing but she told me not to sell crack out of her house and to keep the gang activity away from her house. I did a good job with both. I never had any confrontations at her house and I never had any drug traffic at her house. I did keep my drugs at her house though.

In 2004, I felt my life going downhill in a deep spiral. I was with the mother of my second child. She was living with me, but we didn't get along. We tried to make it work, but the only thing that we had in common was we both like to sell drugs. She was a few years older than me. The first instance I knew my life was getting out of control was a major shootout I had. I've been in shootouts before and I've shot at people, but this time felt different.

I was 20 years old and still in the streets doing the same thing with my life, NOTHING! This particular shootout was over $5.00. I was known in the neighborhood to shoot first and ask questions later. My brother Donta had a confrontation with a guy over $5.00. The guy threatened to shoot my brother the next time he saw him. My brother came and told me to watch out for him and his friends. I took the threat seriously and wanted to look for the guy first. My brother wouldn't let me.

On Mother's Day, the same year, I was cooking Chala (the mother of my child) and my brother Tyrone some breakfast. Donta lived in the apartments directly behind my house. As I was walking down the hallway of my house, I looked out the window and saw the guy that threatened Donta drive past my house towards the apartments. I just knew they were looking for my brother. I ran to the apartments and knocked on the door.

Donta answered and seen the panic on my face and asked, "What's up?"

"Them fools coming your way," I replied.

He grabbed his gun, ran out the house together, and jumped in his car to go back to my house. As we were leaving the apartments, they were turning into the apartment complex. We drove past each other real slow and the driver stuck a pistol out of the window. He pointed it at my brother and I seen him attempt to pull the trigger, but the gun didn't fire right away. I hung out the window and emptied the whole clip from the .45 automatic that I was carrying. Once my brother snapped out the initial shock of almost being shot in the face, he started firing the .357 revolver he had. Once both of our guns were empty, he started to drive off fast to get away from them. I looked back and seen the driver jump out the car and start firing at us with his pistol. I don't know what he was shooting but it seemed like his gun never stopped shooting. I told my brother to get down while grabbing him and pulling him down in the car so we wouldn't get hit. I didn't hear the gun being fired but I did hear the bullets weezing by. That's what happens in a shootout. It's nothing like the movies where you hear a bunch of bang-bang. All you hear is the bullets speed past and the bullet strike what they are striking. The panic of being shot at blocks out the firing of the gun.

We got to my house and he dropped me off. I ran inside and went to reload my gun. When I went back in the front yard to make sure the guys didn't come back down the street to shoot my house up, the police drove up to me without me even seeing them. With me having on some red shorts with a red bandana that signified me as a gang member, I stuck out like a sore thumb. I looked guilty. I tossed my gun in some bushes in front of my house before the police could catch it on me, and tried to act as innocent as possible.

The officer got out of the police car, cuffed me, and then placed me in the car. He then walked directly to my gun and picked it up to smell if it had been fired. My brother pulled up behind the police car and the cop arrested him too. We went to the police station and the cop told us that one of us was going to jail for a long time because the passenger of that car was in the hospital with a gunshot wound to the stomach. I told the officer that I shot the guy. I didn't want my brother to get into any trouble. I've been in and out of jail, and Donta has never even seen a booking area. They took us both to jail for firearm possession, but neither of us was charged with attempted murder like the officer threatened. I later learned that the district attorney deemed it as self-defense, which is not a crime.

I was 20 years old and tired of looking over my shoulders. I had two children on the way and needed to get my life together. In November of 2004, I hit rock bottom.

I was in a huge dispute with Chala. We had been going through a custody battle for my youngest daughter Christajha, who had been taken by the State because of her history with Child Protective Services. Her other four kids were all in state custody and I was just tired of dealing with her. A week before, Chala stole $400.00 from me and some crack. I did not see her for that whole week.

Then suddenly, she called me one morning wanting to talk. I told her we could meet to talk, and so I waited all day for her to come pick me up. She never showed up. I went to the detail shop to wait on her and to be closer to where she was at. She picked me up from the detail shop and we drove off in the car. I was driving the car when she began to complain about the way I was driving, so I told her if she didn't like the way I was driving then she could drive. I pulled over and got out the car. I left the driver door open and walked in front of the car to make it to the passenger side. I thought she was going to walk around too but when I got to the front of the car I saw Chala throw the car in drive. She tried to drive off, almost running me over at the same time. I was thrown onto the hood of the car. I chased the car down, throwing the passenger door open, and we started to fight right there in the parking lot. I jumped in the car and left her there.

I was pissed at the events that just occurred. I figured if she didn't call me and if she stayed where she was then I wouldn't be in this situation. I needed to release some stress, so I wanted to go to the club and party. I stayed in the club, drinking all night long. I drank two bottles of *tequila, 1800*, and two 40 ounces of malt liquor. I was completely inebriated. I never went to sleep that night.

I was pissed at myself early that next morning because I spent too much money in the club that night. All I had was some drugs left, along with a few dollars. I waited until the sun came up so I could catch the city bus to go sell some of my drugs to make up for the foolishness I did the night before. I walked out the apartment that morning, still drinking out of the bottle of liquor that I had, when I saw a woman in a car pull into the parking lot. My first thought was to rob her and take her car so I wouldn't have to ride the bus. That's just what

I did. I pulled out the chrome .357 I was carrying and stuck it in her face. I told her to get out the car, and when she did, I hopped in the car and drove off.

As I exited the apartment complex, I saw the convenience store. I remembered Chala telling me about a confrontation she had with the owner about some clothes she took to have laundered. When she told me about the incident, it always stayed in the back of my mind. When I saw the store, all of that came flooding back into my mind and I wanted to address the confrontation. I walked into the store and pulled the pistol out at the same time. Everything went haywire from there. When he saw me pull out my gun, he hit the alarm and it started to wail real loud. Once I saw him hit the alarm, I saw him grab under the counter. I was scared by then and wanted to get out the store because I thought he was grabbing for his gun. This was just supposed to be a confrontation.

Once I seen him grab under the counter, I fired a shot into the back of the wall on the side of him just to scare him from grabbing anything. He noticed that I didn't shoot him, so he reached under the counter again. I shot him in the hand. When I shot him in the hand, I saw him shake his hand one time and then grab his chest. After that he fell on the ground. I walked out the store, got in the car, and left.

Out of all the crimes I committed in the past, I never had something like this happen to me. I was terrified. I didn't know if he was dead or alive. All I could think was to get out the store without getting shot. To this day, I still think about the stupidity in that decision. All because of a confrontation that he had with Chala; my ego, the fact that I wanted my woman to feel like I had her back and could protect her. This was the same woman that just stole from me a week before. The same woman I just had a huge fight with the night before. The same woman who tried to run me over with the car. It was never my intention to kill that man, let alone shoot him.

I was arrested an hour later. While I was getting interrogated, I found out that he was dead. I was in a state of pure shock. I never killed anyone before. I could not ever say how I felt at that moment when they told me he was dead because my body went numb from the news, and numb from all the liquor I drank. The realization had not set in yet.

CHAPTER 6

I sat in county jail waiting to go to trial for capital murder for fourteen months. I knew I was going to prison for a long time because the attorneys I had would not talk to me.

My attorney came to visit me only one time, and when he did come, he did not mention anything about the trial strategy or any type of investigation he was doing. The questions he asked me told me how he was handling the case. He brought me a message from the district attorney, which was a plea bargain offering two life sentences to avoid trial. He did his best to convince me to take the offer. He told me there was no way he could avoid a death sentence and that he thought the plea bargain would save my life. The attorney said the DA wanted to give me one life sentence for the capital murder and one life sentence for the robbery with the woman in the car. He told me that I would have to serve forty years before I was eligible for parole on the capital murder case. Then <u>if</u> I made parole on that case, I would have to serve another thirty-five years on the robbery case before I was eligible for parole. That was a minimum of seventy-five years in prison. That was the rest of my life and I had just turned 22 years old. I would have been 97 the next possible time I was ready for parole and could see the streets again.

I said to him, "That doesn't sound like a plea bargain. It sounds like a slow death sentence and they are trying to give me that anyway."

There was no way I was signing my life over to the state. I told them if they wanted my life, they would have to take it. I selected my jury on January 22, 2006. The process was long and taxing. I learned a lot through that process. It was at that moment that I saw I was not going to have any say in my own trial. The last form of control that I had was offered to me in the form of two life sentences, and I turned that down and relinquished my say in the rest of the process.

As I went through the process, the two prosecutors, who were both white, showed their strategy very clearly. They wanted to keep all of the African American jurors from the Eastside of San Antonio off the jury, even if it meant violating the law. In 1986, the U.S. Supreme Court ruled in the case of Baton v. Kentucky: "Jurors can not be excluded because of their race." Justice Antoin Scalia expanded on the ruling with: "Jurors can not be excluded due to their religious affiliation."

The prosecutors excluded four Black jurors who were challenged under the 1986 Batson ruling. For one of the jurors, the prosecutor blatantly stated that she was being removed because she was Black. After they stated their main reason, the DA gave three more reasons that were ruled by the judge as "race-neutral."

Another one of the jurors was excluded because of the church she went to. She was asked about her religious views. She told the DA that she went to a church that was located on the Eastside called Victory Outreach. The church did various outreaches in the neighborhood. They had sections of the church that went door-to-door, to homeless shelters and inside the jail to offer outreach to inmates. She was asked if she had ever been inside the jail to do any outreach. She told them no, and stated she wasn't involved with that part of the church; that she only did door-to-door outreach. The DA excluded her anyway, stating that she was involved with the Victory Outreach Church of Christ. We challenged them, stating she testified that she did not go inside the jail and had never been inside the jail. She was fully certified to serve on the jury. Her only problem to the DA was she was Black. She was stricken from the jury.

The third was stricken from the jury because her daughter was charged with grand larceny in South Carolina. The lady told the DA that she knew nothing about the case and had nothing to do with the case. They struck her, saying she had knowledge of the charge. The common denominator of all these women was that they were all Black and from the Eastside of San Antonio. I had a juror that served as a foreman of the jury who had a brother in prison serving time for a rape and murder right here in Texas. The jury gladly accepted him, contradicting themselves and highlighting that the reason they gave for striking one of the jurors was because she was Black. He was Hispanic.

We were done selecting the jury and we ended up with one Black woman who was from the Northside of town, which at the time was considered the upper-class side of town. The rest of the jurors were white and Hispanic, all from the upper-class side of town. The reason I point this out is, according to the law, a defendant is supposed to be judged by a jury of their peers. "Peer" is described in the Merriam-Webster's dictionary as: "Belonging to the same societal group, especially based on age, grade, or status."

None of these jurors were from the same social group as me. None of these twelve jurors were from the same societal group as me. The only thing they knew about young Black males from the Eastside of San Antonio were that the men were thugs and gang members. They didn't understand the dynamics of growing up on that side of town. They didn't understand how hard it was to survive or what it's like watching your mom smoke crack in front of you or how dad beat the hell out of mom or any other hardships we went through. They didn't know or understand how those same hardships can affect a child, teen, or a young man. How could they understand that? They were not my peers. My peers were excluded from my jury simply because they were my peers.

My trial started on February 1, 2006. The DA opened with a dramatic statement of how they were going to show the jury that I killed the victim in cold blood, hunting him down like an animal in the wild. My attorneys opened saying that the State didn't have a case for capital murder because no robbery was conducted. The state called numerous witnesses, mostly forensic experts, to show the bullet wounds, entrance wounds, exit wounds, etc.

Their main witness was the lead detective who investigated the case. He was called to testify in corroboration with the main piece of evidence, a videotape of the murder that was taken from the store's surveillance equipment.

Since the DA knew I didn't take any money or property out the store, to convict me of capital murder they had to prove that I "demanded" money from the victim. To do that, they needed their lead detective to testify that while in the course of his investigation and his viewing of the tape, he heard me demand money from the victim. The videotape was hard to listen to if you were trying to decipher any talking because of the alarm wailing in the background. When the lead detective stepped on the stand, he was asked how many times he had viewed the tape. The detective told the DA he reviewed the tape numerous times after the crime and numerous times directly before testifying. He claimed to be very familiar with the tape. The next question was if he could describe what he heard on the tape. He testified that all he could hear was the wailing of the alarm in the background and that the words were "indecipherable."

That was a major blow to their case. He was the main detective and he couldn't understand the tape. All he said is that he could see that there was a murder. The prosecutor spent a day and a half presenting their case to the jury. When the State rested its case, it was my attorney's turn to present our defense. When the judge asked how much time we needed to prepare, my attorney stood up and told the court that he didn't need any time to prepare because he wasn't going to put up any defense. He rested his case right there. I was in shock. Here I was thinking that he was here to defend me. The DA had just presented all of these fabrications that we could have easily debunked and my attorney still didn't want to fight the case. To this day, I still wonder if he even had a defense ready or was prepared to fight the case. I don't think he did.

Right before the jury was sent to deliberate they had to be presented with the rules of law and a charge to convict me under. The charge they were given was capital murder or acquittal. My attorneys argued that the DA didn't prove that I robbed or attempted to rob the victim. Since they failed to prove any robbery, a charge of felony murder, murder, and manslaughter should be entered into the jury charge so the jury can decide which one to convict me under, if I was going to be convicted. Felony murder was an automatic life sentence. Murder carried 5-99 years or a life sentence, and manslaughter was anywhere from 2-20 years. The judge denied the charges and left the jury with the charge of capital murder or acquittal. I knew I was going to jail for a long time. There was no way a jury was going to acquit me of that murder after seeing me on that videotape, no matter the circumstances.

After about an hour and a half of deliberations, the jury came back with a guilty verdict for capital murder. It was time for the second part of my trial, the punishment phase; the phase that would determine life or death. The punishment phase was not any different from the first two parts of these sham proceedings. My life was put on trial that day with no understanding of why I did what I was doing throughout my life and the history of the incidents. This is where having a jury of my peers was crucial. The assault on my mother was brought up, the burglary charge, and the incident where I was accused of beating up a San Antonio Police Officer.

I was driving a car that my friend had come to my house in. It was a stick shift. He rented it from a crack user, trading some crack cocaine. I asked him if he had paid for the car so they wouldn't call it in stolen. He told me that he did pay them, and we had the car for the entire day so I went riding around. We were smoking weed and I had drugs on me at the time. When the officer tried to pull us over, I drove off on him so I could try to get rid of the drugs and to give me room to jump out and run, which I eventually did. He called a helicopter to assist in the pursuit. I ran under a bridge thinking I could get out of the helicopter's line of sight. He followed me and put the gun to my head once he had caught up to me. He told me to lay on the ground. I did and he handcuffed me. Once I was in cuffs, he started to beat me up. He punched me in the face numerous times, kneed me in the side, and then dragged me from under the bridge all the way down the street where his car was. I was fucked up. My face was swollen, cut and it had dried blood on it. My shirt was even ripped.

At the trial, that same police officer took the stand to testify on how I beat him up. I asked my attorney to pull the arrest photo from that day to show who beat up whom. I knew the photo would show the wounds and how my face was swollen. He ignored me like he usually did. The prosecutor also introduced the jury to the shooting I had with the individuals in the apartments. The judge didn't want them to bring it up in front of the jury because I was never charged with a crime. He said that since I wasn't charged with a crime they couldn't allege that I had committed one. The way they got around his ruling was that I was caught with a gun that day. They wanted to bring up that I was caught with a .45 automatic, which they had in the courtroom. To do that they had to bring up the shooting, since it was all in the same incident. They maneuvered out of that ruling and told the jury how I shot an individual with that gun and how I tried to run from the police that same day. Not once did they bring up how I was defending myself. I asked the attorney to call the individual that I was in the shootout with to the stand, and told him that they would testify that I didn't start the confrontation. He ignored that also.

My attorney brought up his mitigating evidence: the rape of my sister, the murder of my father and the instability of my upbringing. He addressed all of these issues in a dry and removed manner. He didn't give a fuck! After the "defense," the jury was again instructed and sent to deliberate my fate. This time there were no arguments about charges or definitions of the law. There were only two choices for them to make: LIFE or DEATH. The jurors needed a little bit longer this time. Nobody knows why or what the conversation was about behind those doors, but they took almost five hours. They came back with my fate: DEATH!

I was sentenced to the death penalty on February 7, 2006. My whole body went numb. My mind went blank. Although I knew that death was a possibility, I never attempted to prepare myself for that outcome. How can a person prepare themselves to hear they are about to die? What was I to do at that moment? I didn't hear my mother faint in the courtroom at the same time the judge told me words that I will never forget; words that registered in my consciousness even though I was lost.

"May God Have Mercy On Your Soul!"

I was only 22 years old.

CHAPTER 7

I was laying in my cell one night in the county jail when a voice came over the intercom,

"Young, you are on the TDC chain. Pack up. You are going to death row!"

I was ready to leave. It was March 31, 2006 and I had been in the county jail for sixteen months. I already had my death sentence and was tired of living in that county jail cell. I packed up my belongings as quickly as I could and I was ready to go. I was shackled up and placed in a squad car. We hit the highway on our way to Huntsville, TX.

Death row prisoners are housed at *Polunsky Unit* in Livingston, Texas, but the death chamber is at the famous *Walls Unit* in Huntsville, TX. The *Walls Unit* is the oldest unit in Texas and it is located in downtown Huntsville. The drive was long but welcoming. I enjoyed looking at the surroundings passing by. The farm country was new to me. I lived in the city my whole life. I thought to myself that this was the last chance I would ever see this type of scenery. I wanted to take as much of it in as I could and hold on to it to think of later.

Four hours after leaving San Antonio, we arrived at the *Bird Unit* which is an intake unit. I saw white uniforms moving around freely, washing buses, washing cars, and engaged in all types of other activities. I never saw inmates with so much freedom. I thought to myself that I could do this prison time. It is nothing but time and I've been doing time since I was 11 years old. I was taken inside the prison and placed inside a big cage. As soon as the cuffs were off, a correctional officer (C.O.) came up to me and started barking orders. I just stood there looking at him. Not because I didn't want to listen, but because I didn't understand a word he was saying to me. He had a country drawl so strong that most of his words were drawn out real long. He then spoke to me in the prison lingo that I wasn't accustomed to yet, and he had a huge wad of chewing tobacco jammed inside his cheeks. Once he saw that I didn't move, he stepped closer to the cage and said, "Boi, did you hair a word eyes jus said to youuuu?"

I told him, "No," shaking my head at the same time.

He said, "I said, come'on out doze clothes and do dat dance fo' me. Eyes noze diz ain't yo first rodeo, iz it?"

I stripped and did a quick spin. I'm not a big fan of dancing for anybody but I knew what he wanted me to do.

"What the fuck waz dat, boi? Follow my instructions and wez can get diz here shit over with. Runz yoz fingers though yoz hair. Now lift up doz arms. That's good, youz doing good, boi. Now open up dat mouth and runz yoz fingers inside dat jawline. Now lift up thoz nuts. Turn around, bend over, and spread thoz cheeks. Now lift up both feet. Good boi, see that wasn't hard, waz it?"

He then threw me a brown paper bag and some boxer shorts and told me, "Get doz draws on and get some of dat dere good salami in you. We will deal wit you in a sec."

I opened up the brown sack after putting the boxers on and saw four salami and cheese sandwiches inside. I was so hungry that once I saw them, my stomach started talking to me. I didn't want to eat because I didn't want to take my eyes off my surroundings, so I went to the back of the cage and placed my back against the wall so I could keep my eye on everything. I scarfed those sandwiches down. They were good, the best thing that I'd eaten in sixteen months.

He then shackled me up and took me to get fingerprinted and get my picture taken. I quickly understood why everybody's mugshot looked bad. The inmate is always tired from lack of sleep and when the picture is snapped it is always snapped at the wrong time.

Once we were done with that process I was taken back to the area with the cage and given some white prison clothes that were a size too big. After that, I was shackled again and led to a van that was waiting outside. I asked where we were going and the officers looked at me like I was from another planet and told me, "Death row." I thought we were on death row, but it seemed I got one last chance to see the scenery and enjoy the surroundings.

Polunsky Unit wasn't that long of a drive away, about thirty minutes. As we drove down the road along the side of the unit, I saw the sprawling landscape around the building and the imposing electric fence around one of its buildings. One of the C.O.s saw me looking at it and said, "That's death row. That's where you are going."

I guess he thought that I needed to be reminded of that fact. We pulled to the first guard shack and the van was checked for any contraband that could have been hidden inside. We were cleared to enter and we pulled up to the back gate. I was let out of the van there to a huge welcoming committee. The way I was shackled made it hard for me to walk. I was hunched over and the shackles on my feet were so close that I could only take baby steps to avoid falling.

When I entered the building that housed death row, I was taken to a small room where the welcoming committee, which consisted of about ten officers ranking from Major down to the Sergeant, ogled me like I was an animal at the zoo. I didn't know if all of them were there to help with the intake process or just to see the new arrival, but I found out fifteen minutes later when half of them disappeared. I was stripped searched again as if I had the chance to hide something while I was chained up. Then I was given a pair of boxers. These were no ordinary boxers. These boxers had no elastic. They were held together by two strings on each side which were to be tied to each other and a small piece of Velcro in the front. When I got them, I stepped into them but I didn't know how to make them fit. I've never seen anything like them before.

I asked the officer who was watching me dress, "How do I put these on?"

"I don't know, I don't have to wear them," he responded.

I did the best I could and had them held up to where they wouldn't fall down when I walked. The guards took me to my cell, and I walked inside and stood there, taking it all in. I saw a metal bed running along the back wall and two metal tables sticking out from the side of the wall about two and a half feet on top of each other, with a three-foot space separating the two. I also saw a stainless steel toilet/sink combination mounted along a wall. That wall also had a big fluorescent light, a two plug outlet, and a button mounted on it that controlled the light. Looking outside the door, I saw the full pod that I was housed on. Each pod had six different sections positioned in a U-shape with a viewing post (picket) in the middle for the C.O.s. Each section had fourteen cells, seven on the top row and seven on the bottom row. The shower was at the end of each row on each section. There was also a dayroom on each section that was surrounded with bars, a pull up bar, stainless steel table and a toilet/sink combo inside of it. Each pod also had two separate recreation yards that were enclosed by three walls and a big window for the C.O.s to see through. Each rec yard had two sides, both sides containing a pull-up bar, toilet and sink, and a basketball goal. The sides were separated by a long row of bars where each inmate could shake hands through. There was an opening in the roof enclosed in bars, but with the sky visible.

I was tired but my adrenaline was rushing at the same time. I was running through stories that I was told from friends who served time. I was thinking about the ways I should conduct myself, how to listen for certain signs of danger, and how to get respect. They also told me that respect is the golden ticket to survival in prison. While I was standing there, I heard a knock on the wall.

"What's up?" I answered.

"What do they call you?" The voice said.

"They call me Lunatik," I responded, telling him the name I picked up in the county jail for being a knucklehead and rascal.

"Well, Lunatik, they call me Max."

"How do you turn these lights off? It's bright as fuck," I asked Max.

"There should be a button on the wall that you can push and it will turn it off."

I did and the bright light went out, leaving the sun shining through a small window that was at the top of the cell. The window was about one foot from the ceiling and was a long slit running horizontal along the wall.

"You are going to need to clean that cell out. I am going to send you some cleaning supplies. Plus, there are going to be people sending you other stuff," Max said out of nowhere.

"I will take some cleaning supplies but I don't want anything else," I said. In prison you are taught not to accept anything from anybody because there are always strings attached. I have heard stories where a kid that just arrived to prison was offered a cigarette from an inmate. Once the kid finished smoking the cigarette, the inmate told him, "I want my cigarette back."

The kid, thinking the inmate wanted to get paid for his cigarette, told the inmate that he would give him it back once his mom sends him some money.

The inmate told him, "I want THAT cigarette back!"

That is the kind of games that inmates play when you let them give you things in prison. I refused to fall in that trap.

Max then said, "Look, Youngster, you are not going to have anything for a few months. Everybody here knows that. Nobody wants anything back and nobody is going to play any of the games that you are thinking of. It's cool to take the stuff."

I told him, "okay" because I knew that would stop him from talking. I was standing around when I saw a jar slide into my cell through a hole at the bottom of the door. I jumped, not knowing what the hell was going on and not knowing where it was coming from.

I heard Max say, "Can you get that?"

I told him yes, and that I had received it. He said for me to keep it all because the guy who lived in the cell before me was nasty and he used to play in his shit and rub it all over the walls. I looked inside the jar and saw it was filled with soap and scouring powder. I started to clean the cell up, scrubbing the walls. Yes, that cell was filthy. I heard something hit the ground outside my cell door, so I stopped what I was doing. I went to look and see what it was and I saw a string hanging from the second floor with a small weight attached to it. As I stood there and watched, Max shot a line with a pole attached to it across the one hanging over the rails on the row above. The pole he had attached had a few hooks on the end so when he pulled it back, it grabbed the line he had crossed. He pulled it inside his cell and then yelled to the owner of the line upstairs that he had it. Then a voice came back and told him to pull the line. Max started to pull the line and packages started coming over the railing. Pack after pack was being pulled into Max's cell. I sat there entranced by what I was seeing. Of all the time that I've been locked up I've never seen anything like it. Once Max had pulled everything into his cell, he yelled to the guy upstairs that he had everything and for him to pull his line back. Then I saw the line being pulled back and eventually disappear back upstairs. I went back to cleaning my cell when I heard something slide inside my cell again. I turned around to look and it was Max's pole. He said, "Pull the line." I did and the same packs that I seen being pulled over the railings were entering my cell. Once I was done, I had over fifteen packs of items inside my cell. Everything from hygiene to food. I had it all. I just took it all and stacked it by the door. I had no plans on using any of it. There was no way I was getting caught up in any of the penitentiary games. I finished cleaning up the cell and laid down. I was so exhausted that I dozed off fast.

CHAPTER 8

Before I arrived on Texas death row, the thought of the death penalty never crossed my mind. I grew up in an environment where going to the penitentiary was like a badge of acceptance. I knew I was going to end up in prison one day. The gang activity I was engaged in was going to land me there. I didn't care at the time. Ever since my Uncle Michael ended up in prison, I knew I had to go to gain the same status as he did. He is considered a legend in the hood and I wanted to be the same. He was my idol. The stories I heard about prison were the ones of power, masculinity and respect, no matter how they have to be obtained.

Prison is a dog eat dog world. There is every type of mentality known to man here. Every type of characteristic is here. When dealing with the individuals, one has to always be on guard or become a victim to one of the various schemes that are conducted on a daily basis. Death row was completely different. All of the stigmas, the jackets and the labels that death row has didn't fit. The care packages that I received on my first day here were just a glimpse of the characteristics that death row has. That has been a part of death row tradition for well over twenty years. You will never find a gesture like that in general population anywhere in Texas, and Texas has over 125 prisons.

I was on death row for a few days when around 11:45 a.m., Max hit on the wall and told me to look out of the window. The view I had was of the back intake gate where I just arrived days before. When I looked out the window, I saw a small Texas Department of Corrections (TDC) van back up to the gate with a bunch of plainclothes individuals standing around shaking hands, patting each other on the back, smiling and laughing with one another.

I asked him, "What is going on out there?"

He just told me to watch and see. A few minutes later I saw an inmate walking down the walkway coming from the visitation room. He was the leader of a mass of other spectators including a six-man, fully equipped riot team with wheelchair and gurney (just in case the inmate did not comply) and numerous other guards. It seemed to be twenty officers in all. I still didn't know what was going on. I figured there must have been a riot or something similar to it. I didn't ask Max any more questions. I continued to watch the scene play out. The inmate was escorted back inside the building that housed death row.

Five minutes later he was brought back out, chained and shackled, then led to the waiting van. Once he was secured inside the van, three plainclothes officials jumped inside with him and they drove away.

Once the scene was over, I asked my neighbor, "What the hell was all of that?"

Max replied, "He has an execution date and they are taking him to the *Walls Unit* where the execution chamber is at."

I was stunned. I've only been on death row a few days and I have just seen one man being led to his own slaughter. I didn't know what to think. Was I next? That was the only question that I could only think of. My mind was flooded with questions along those lines that I didn't know if I wanted answered. On that day, that same inmate was executed. That day, I learned that although I lived around a lot of good hearted people, the State of Texas was executing them without a conscience.

Ten months of me being on death row, I was on the outside recreation yard and the C.O.s went inside my cell. I had just learned the quick process on how to make wine (hooch). I had five bottles brewing in the back of my cell. They found them and took them to their superiors. Distilling alcohol was a disciplinary infraction. I was written a disciplinary case and taken to level. Level is located in another housing unit (pod).

All inmates on death row start off classified as level 1 offenders. Level 1 is the level where you get the most "privileges." Whenever we get any major disciplinary cases, we get downgraded to level 2 or 3. Both levels are located on what we call "F-pod." F-pod is known for chaos. At any given moment of the day you may have a bomb-fire blazing, a gassing going on or any other type of disruptions there. When the guards walked me down the hallway I turned the corner to enter the pod door and could smell the recent fire that had just been extinguished. It barely masked the smell of shit that lingered in the air. When entering F-pod, it was dark with a somber feeling inside it. It seemed like being in jail. I was placed in a cell with no paint on the walls and the light had only one bulb that worked.

On first sight I could tell these cells had been neglected, maintenance wise. I went to the dayroom the next day and started doing my workout. I didn't know anyone on the pod and wasn't looking to make any new friends.

I heard a voice call out, "Look out, Dayroom."

"What's up?" I responded.

"What they call you?" the voice said.

"Lunatik."

"I am C-loc. I am down here in 74 cell."

"Where are you from?" I asked.

"The Southeast side of San Antonio" he responded.

My ears perked up once I heard my city being named. I told him I was from the Eastside of San Antonio. A special bond was born that day, one that would take me a while to appreciate. Reginald "Omari/C-loc" Blanton was a blessing in disguise for me. When I met Reginald he had been on death row for five years and was fully aware of the way the murder machine worked. I was still green at the time, although I had seen a few executions by then. Reginald had these gold-framed Gianni Versace frames on his face and two gold teeth. He was very stocky around the chest and arms, which came from the years of being in juvenile and the Texas Youth Commission (TYC, the Youth Prison of

Texas). He was also a "37 L.O.C. Crip," which was a rival of mine. When I met him I never had any intentions of becoming his friend. There was too much friction between our gangs, and I wanted to stay on guard just in case we had to clash. I was still in my street mindset then. Reginald's intentions were different. He seen something in me that I never took the time out to see for myself. He saw potential to do something great. So he made the first attempt at friendship.

The day after I met Reginald he sent me a book titled *Breaking the Chains of Psychological Slavery* by Naim Akbar. The book talked about the Black man and the way he acted and how the way he acted contributed to the acts that were forced on Blacks during slavery. He gave firm examples of numerous acts and how over the years the Black man has been institutionalized from the days of slavery.

I read the book, although I didn't want to admit it. It spoke directly to the ways I carried myself. That book opened up floodgates for me. I returned it back to Omari and asked him if he had anything else along the same lines. He introduced me to all types of individuals over the years: Huey P. Newton, Bobby Seale and Eldridge Cleaver of the Black Panther Party; Fredrick Douglas, Malcolm X and Martin Luther King Jr. of the Civil Rights movements; and Karl Marx and Fredrick Engels. This process wasn't as easy as it sounds. Although I loved what he had me reading, I was still a stubborn, combative kid. I would argue with him, but Omari was very patient with me. He was patient by nature. He didn't get frustrated or mad with me when I would debate and argue with him. He would just make his point by sending me another book.

During the three months I was on F-pod, I was introduced to the D.R.I.V.E. (Death Row Inner-Communalist Vanguard Engagement). Omari was a part of the group. The group consisted of individuals who protested the inhumane living conditions that plagued death row. They utilized numerous tactics, i.e. sit-ins, hunger strikes and direct action (gassing just to name a few) to get their voices heard and to bring these conditions to light. I watched them get so much done and I knew I wanted to help them in any way I could. Omari introduced me to Gabriel "Capone" Gonzalez. Capone was also from San Antonio. I knew Capone. Before he came to death row he was a legend in the streets. He was a "357 Crip" and notorious on the Eastside. He and my Uncle Michael were huge enemies. I immediately did not like Capone.

When I met Capone he had been on death row for thirteen years and didn't engage in any gang activity anymore. He took me outside where it was just the two of us. He told me the things we did on the streets were to be left on the streets. We were both here on death row, fighting for our lives. To engage in that senseless activity was giving the State of Texas a huge win in the quest to murder us. I listened very closely because even though he was a rival of mine, he was also an O.G. (Original

Gangster) in the neighborhood and it was an honor just speaking to him. Once we cleared all of our beef and made a pact to fight for our lives together, assisting each other any way we could, another bond was formed.

I did my ninety days for my infraction and was sent back to level 1. My life was changed and I didn't know it. Level 1 wasn't the same to me anymore. I started to notice all of the inhumane conditions and unjust treatment. I had to go back to F-pod and assist D.R.I.V.E. in the fight. I lasted thirty days when I voluntarily went back to level 2 by telling officers that I refused to go back inside my cell. I was on F-pod again, and I asked Omari what I had to do to assist. They went through a voting process that confirmed my membership in the movement, and I was taught numerous tactics to use while dealing with the administration. One of the biggest things I was taught was communication.

Omari and Capone taught me that we were not to engage the administration as if they were the enemy, but as if they were human beings, which in turn humanized you. It took me a while to learn this tactic since I always looked at C.O.s as the police and not as human beings that went home daily to their families. Once I learned this tactic and learned how to talk to the administration, it was an eye opener for me. I learned a lot of the C.O.s did not agree with what was being done to us, how we were being housed, the way we were treated and the living conditions we were subjected to on a daily basis. Their only problem was they did not have the power and/or voice to change it. They secretly supported our actions. This tactic proved fail-proof.

In addition to learning how to communicate with the administration, I also learned how to combat the gas. Gas is the repressive mechanism that TDC uses, not only as a control measure, but also as a scare mechanism. It comes in a 14 oz can that resembles a mini fire extinguisher, and not only does it burn the skin on contact, it takes all of the oxygen out of the air in the attempt to interrupt the breathing. At this time, gas was a major obstacle to overcome. If I learned to overcome the gas, I would survive in the fight to change the conditions that we lived in.

I had my first gassing on July 24, 2007. It started on July 22 when I decided to protest an execution date of a fellow inmate. I went on the outside recreation yard and refused to come off. I was not planning on letting them gas me. I only wanted to conduct a sit-in and let the administration know that we did not agree with the murder of our fellow inmate. The Sergeant came to ask me what was going on and why I refused to come off the rec yard.

"What's the problem, Young?"

"The problem is y'all are killing us without thoroughly looking at every aspect of our cases," I replied.

"Young, we have no control over the way the courts handle y'all's cases. We just house y'all," he responded.

"Well, the way y'all house us is another issue. The living conditions are inhumane. The food is not edible. The dayrooms are filthy from the numerous gassings and them not being cleaned afterwards. I can go on and on, but you know all of this so there is no point in wasting much time. I am not coming out, so suit your team up and come get me," I said.

He knew I was new to the movement. They also knew I had not taken the gas before, so they had no problem doing just that; suiting up a riot team. Knowing the way they interacted with each other, they probably made a wager to see if I was going to come out or not. Whoever bet that I was not was going to lose because I just planned to conduct a simple sit-in. They came with a five-man riot team and numerous spectators. The outside rec yard has a huge picture window, so it was more than enough room for everybody to crowd around and watch the show. The ones that bet I was their race horse were up at the starting blocks. The Sergeant stepped on the rec yard with a military gas mask on his face and a can of gas in his hand. Obviously, he was ready to gas the hell out of me if it came to that. He gave me two direct orders with the camera rolling.

"Young, submit to proper strip search and the application of hand restraints or chemical agents will be utilized."

"I cannot do that, Sarg," I replied.

"Young, this is your second order. Submit to the application of hand restraints and the proper strip search or chemical agents will be utilized."

I then started to strip. I went through the full strip search process. Once I was done, I was placed in handcuffs and walked to the other side of the red yard where I sat down. I did this so they had to carry me back to my cell as far as I could make them. They came, picked me up, and carried me to my cell.

Once I was in my cell, the Major, who is head of security and the highest ranking officer under the Warden, came to my cell and said, "You are a pussy. You got that pussy so go sit your pussy on your bunk and go wipe your little wet pussy, and when I shut this D.R.I.V.E. bullshit down I am going to blame it all on you."

I smiled at her but inside I was seething. I haven't been talked to like that in a long time. I knew I couldn't say anything back to her because from her unprofessional response, I knew I won the battle and the action I took was effective. Maybe she bet that I would stay on the yard and get gassed. We let her and her crew leave. I made the decision that the next time I stepped out of my cell I was going to make administration gas me. I knew in order for them to take my protest seriously, I had to overcome their chemical agents. I told the rest of the members my decision. They argued that I couldn't be reactive to her comments. I rebutted their arguments, stating that her comments will continue verbally or through her actions if I don't show her what I am doing is not a game or for show. So, I had to do something. The good thing about the group is we used to engage in debates that looked at every angle we could find for our actions. We tried to look at the consequences of our actions to be ready for the outcome and prepare ourselves on how to deal with it.

After hours of debate, my mind was made up and I was going to protest the unprofessionalism of the Major. In turn, I was taking on the top of the administration.

When the day came, I went to the dayroom fully ready for anything that may come. I had all the necessary materials, which consisted of a strip of plastic to cover my eyes, a sheet to make an improvised gas mask, and a jumper to keep the gas off my body. Once it was time for the dayroom's two-hour time block to end, the officers came to place me back in my cell, but of course, I refused like I did in the rec yard. The officer went through the same process of calling the ranking officials. Two Sergeants came to talk to me. When they saw me, they knew that talking would be futile. I was ready with all the equipment on. I had a ball of toilet paper in my hand.

I walked up the bars, sat the toilet paper down and told the Sergeants, "Tell the Major to come wipe my wet pussy!"

They shook their heads, understanding the innuendo fully. They walked off and suited up their riot team. When they came back they had two cans of gas and a long gun, but no Major. I have never seen the gun before and I didn't know what it did. It was long and resembled a shotgun, 12-gauge. The hole of the barrel looked like it could shoot out a tennis ball. One Sergeant pointed the gun at me and gave me the same two orders that they gave me two days before. I refused both of them, this time knowing I was going to have to get gassed. After the two orders, I heard a loud blast. I jumped from the sound and a huge cloud of smoke hit me in the face. The Sergeant had fired the gun. The other Sergeant sprayed the can of gas directly at me, emptying it in one blast. They waited three minutes for the chemicals to take effect and see if I would submit. Once the three minutes was up, they sprayed me with the second can.

During the entire time of me being gassed, I was trying to control my breathing. The main thing to do when dealing with the gas is trying not to cough. I could feel a tingle in my throat and a tickle in my nose. I knew not to cough, though. If I was to cough, the gas would attack my respiratory system and interrupt my breathing. After another three minutes, the Sergeant lined up the five-man riot team at the dayroom door. They gave me one last order to come out. I refused again. They opened the door and the riot team came in to get me. A riot team is made up of five or more men all weighing over 200 pounds. They have on knee pads, elbow pads, a shank proof vest, a helmet and a military grade gas mask. They are also equipped with a fiberglass capture shield. It is a sight to see to have over 1000 pounds coming at you full force. I panicked at first like a deer caught in the headlights, but quickly regained my composure and scuffled with the team for almost a minute, which is a long time in a fight. They got me on the ground and took me back to my cage. The Major never did come to talk to me again.

CHAPTER 9

I grew a lot during my time of protesting. The group members would hold daily study sessions on various subjects. We understood how we were perceived by the general public and wanted to combat that by continuing to grow and educate ourselves. One of our major forms of protest was conducting sit-ins on execution dates. We wanted to show the inmate who had the date that he wasn't alone in the fight for his life. We also wanted the world to know that we were not in agreement at all with the state sanctioned murders that were being conducted.

I remember it was in September of 2007, and the State of Texas had three murders scheduled back-to-back. I refused to let an event like that go without a statement being made. I went to the visitation room for a visit on a Saturday. Two of the individuals had already been executed days before and the last individual was left for the next week.

When my visit was over and I was being escorted back to my cell, I stepped out of the visitation room onto the breezeway that led back to my building. The breezeway is a narrow space that is enclosed by a chain-link fence. It is about 100 yards from the visitation room to the building. I knew if I conducted my protest right outside the visitation room it would be very effective for two reasons:

1.) That was the same walk that the inmate with the date takes when he is led to the van to be taken to the death chamber at the *Walls Unit*.

2.) I knew that the guards would have to carry me as far as possible since the cell I was housed in was in the back of the death row building.

When I walked out of the visitation room, I sat on the ground. I refused to walk. I told the escorting officers to get a ranking official so I could be on a gurney back to my cell. A ranking officer came from the general population with the demeanor that they use for the inmates that have little time to go. He stepped directly in my face, close enough to where I could smell the freshly smelling chewing tobacco in his cheek, and told me, "Get the fuck off my run, Boi!"

I smiled at him. I understood how the game works and I understood what he was trying to do. He wanted a response to justify the beating he had on his mind for the disobedience I was engaging in. What he got was a response that he did <u>not</u> expect.

I said to him, with a smile on my face and in a calm tone, "From my understanding, you do not own this prison. Secondly, according to the PD-22, your handbook for the rules that an officer must follow, rule 14 states: *An officer is not supposed to use any type of profanity or racial language to an offender/client. If the offender/client uses it to the officer first, the officer is not supposed to respond in a like manner.* I also know the use of force procedure. If you would like me to quote that also, I have no problems doing so OR you can go get your camera and the gurney and we can get this protest on its way."

He stood there with a baffled look on his face. I knew he had never been talked to that way and he didn't know how to respond to it. A voice pulled him out of his stumper telling him that they will take over from there. It was a female Sergeant that dealt with protest on a continuous basis. She asked me, "Is this another peaceful protest, Young?"

"It sure is, Sarg, and I am ready when you are ready," I replied.

She got on her walkie-talkie and told the voice on the other side to bring a wheelchair. I stopped her to tell her that I refused to willingly ride in a wheelchair like I am a patient and that she might as well call for a gurney. I wanted to gurney as part of my protest. The gurney was a prop that I had been planning to use to make my statement more effective. I also wanted the inmates to know that in this protest we are willing to ride the gurney with them.

When they brought the gurney along, I had more spectators than usual. Most of the officers that came to watch were officers that worked with the general population inmates, and although they have heard about the protests occurring on death row, they never saw it for themselves. This was their chance. I was hoisted onto the gurney like numerous others before me. A camera was rolling and I made sure I explained each step of the use of force process and how it was exactly the same as the execution protocol. When I was strapped down I made sure to point out that in solidarity, I am being strapped down like the numerous others that have been executed by the state. I was wheeled to my cell and stripped naked. All of my clothes were taken from me. I was left in a cell naked for the rest of the night.

This protest reverberated throughout death row. It did a lot to reinvigorate the ones that had execution dates and didn't feel that anyone understood what they were really going through. They now knew that, not only did we understand them, we cared. That was also my first time being strapped to a gurney, but it certainly wasn't my last.

The protest went on like that for all of 2007. In October 2007, D.R.I.V.E. scored a major victory against the killing machine. Kenneth "Haramia" Foster, who was a member, had an execution date for August 20th. He was on death row for a murder that he did not commit and the State of Texas knew this. They sent him to death row under the "*Law of Parties*" rule; a rule that states that if a person is at the scene of the crime with the actual killer, he or she is just as responsible for the murder as if they pulled the trigger themselves. Kenneth was well over hundred feet away from the murder and did not know what was going on at the time of the crime.

Kenneth was sitting in the driver's seat of his car waiting on a friend. He heard gunshots and saw his friend running back to the car, yelling that he was being shot at, and for Kenneth to hurry up and drive. Kenneth did what any sane individual would have done. He got the hell out of there! He was later picked up for the murder. He was put on trial in the same courtroom and at the same time as the actual killer which made him look like he had something to do with the murder. Once his co-defendant was convicted of capital murder, he was also. Both were sentenced to death. Kenneth went on a major campaign to save his life. He wanted to expose the law of parties as a law that executed innocent men; a law that was used to justify the tough-on-crime mantra that Texas lives by. He had people from all over the world that latched on to his plight. They continuously repeated that he didn't need to be executed with so much uncertainty surrounding his conviction. The movement attracted numerous political figures, along with influential figures across the world.

While Kenneth had the outside campaign going, D.R.I.V.E. had the inside campaign fired up. One thing that we taught one another was that the fight inside fed the fight outside and vice versa. Nobody was going to fight for us if we didn't fight for ourselves. We conducted sit-ins every time that we stepped out of our cells. We conducted so many sit-ins that the administration stopped writing us disciplinary cases because the paperwork was too overwhelming. They started using tactics that we had never seen before. They went seven full days without letting us go out of our cells for anything. This meant no showers, no recreation, and even tried to deny our visits. We still found ways to get our voices heard and continued to protest. The day Kenneth was scheduled to be executed, the

D.R.I.V.E. members were placed on a security lockdown, which meant we could not have our tray slots open for any reason, and in turn, could not eat that day. We didn't care because we did not plan to eat that day anyway. We had already planned a hunger strike to show solidarity to our brother who planned to deny his last meal. We did have attorney visits set up so we could all be in the visitation room with him before he left the unit.

The administration pulled a fast one on everybody, inside and out. They transported Kenneth in the middle of the night to the *Walls Unit* without the knowledge of any of his family members. Kenneth was waiting on a ruling from Rick Perry, the Governor of Texas, to grant him clemency or to carry out the murder. Kenneth had received a rare ruling from the *Board of Pardons and Paroles* that approved the clemency, which would give him a life sentence. Rick Perry had political decisions to make, one that was delicate, but could not be avoided. The decision he would make would define the rest of his career as a politician.

Of course, he had seen Arnold Schwarzenegger in California when he was Governor and had to deal with the execution of Stanley "Tookie" Williams. Williams was the founder of the street gang the "Crips," but was also nominated for a Nobel Peace Prize for the numerous children's books he had written. He also negotiated a détente between the Bloods and the Crips, and wrote his own autobiography all while sitting on death row. Schwarzenegger still executed him and committed political suicide at the same time. Perry had to tread lightly. What he needed to do was find a way to appease both sides of the spectrum, which both had his constituents on them.

When he held his press conference, hair stiff and in place like it always was, he announced his decision to grant clemency to Kenneth. Perry's decision was due to the way Kenneth's trial was conducted; him being tried at the same time as his co-defendant. He went on to say that those types of trials had to be stopped and looked into. He said that each defendant was entitled to his or her own trial. He never mentioned the law of parties, which was what had everybody divided in the first place. The way Perry addressed the situation was brilliant. He pleased both sides of the debate. The advocates for the law of parties to stay on the books were fine with the decision because it didn't affect the law. Those advocating for Kenneth were satisfied because he got to live. He never did address the issues of joint trials again.

With Kenneth getting his life sentence, we were inspired. The blood, sweat and tears we were putting into the anti-death penalty and prison reform movement meant something. The administration asked us to please calm down with the protest and give them a chance to address the complaints that we were bringing to their attention. We all calmed down to focus on our personal and legal situation. Gabriel was looking to receive a life sentence due to a discrepancy at his trial. (He eventually got the life sentence.) Reginald watched his case get kicked out of the Federal Courts due to the incompetence of his attorneys, and I was dealing with the incompetence of the appeals attorney that I had at the time.

CHAPTER 10

It was getting towards the end of 2008, and death row was moving along without any major incidents. The administration did what they could to address the issues that we brought to their attention and things were as smooth as it could get for the person living on death row. The killing machine never stopped taking its victims and there was nothing we could do about that. It was an inevitable occurrence that we learned to deal with the best way we could.

In October 2008, a major scandal hit death row, one that would reverberate across the nation and affect every prison in America. Contraband cell phones in prison had been around for years. The prison system turned a blind eye to them like they've done every other black market venture that feeds the inmate economy. Nothing major happened before with the use of illegal cell phones, so why would the prison system open themselves up to ridicule when they could hear no evil, see no evil and speak no evil? That was about to end.

In the same month, October, a death row inmate used a contraband cell phone to contact a State Senator of Texas with the hopes of getting some political help on his case. The inmate was not the sharpest pencil in the box and did not know the fire he was stepping into. When the Senator balked at the inmate's request, the inmate switched tactics and tried to threaten his family. This was the wrong thing to do. This sent a shock wave through death row that we still feel to this day and will always feel. Death row was placed on a very intense lock-down and subjected to a thorough shakedown. The lockdown lasted two long and hard months. This was a depressing time for us. Throughout the entire two months, no more than three or four cell phones turned up from the search. Investigations from every acronym in the government were conducted. TDC used the attention to show the rigorous security measures they were putting into place. Inmates that had high profile cases were back in the spotlight even if they had nothing to do with the cell phones. It was utter chaos. The debate for cell phone jammers in every prison was on.

In prison, the inmate had very little freedom let alone access to things of the modern world i.e. cell phones, laptops, tablets, etc. General population offenders do have freedom to work, go to school, and watch television. Every death row in America has access to television, except the men on Texas death row. The women that are housed on a different part of the state had access to TV. Texas death row males have nothing. We are locked in our cells 22-23 hours of the day, and allowed a 15-minute phone call every ninety days, only <u>if</u> the request is granted.

TDC is a state run institution which is funded by state grant money. This gave the state power to have an oversight committee that has the say of what is sold to the prisoner and what is not. Even with numerous outcries of officers who work death row daily wanting death row inmates to have TVs, the committee has constantly ignored their request. Deaf ears like these created the black market for cell phones. Texas recently passed a bill in 2009 that gave prisoners access to payphones. The bill did not cover death row. Death row is being punished for the embarrassment that the inmate gave TDC.

In November 2008, I received a letter that five individuals who were on my visitation list were being removed because of a "security concern." The individuals were: my mother, my youngest brother, my grandfather, my cousin, and my friend. Three of the individuals have never been on the unit.

They claimed I called them on a contraband phone, which I did. I was never caught with the cell phone. I knew that my calling them was not the reason they were taking them off the list. A majority of the inmates on death row were using cell phones that were confiscated, but very few of them had anybody taken off their list. When I talked to an official in the administration about the issue, I was told it was because my family didn't report me to them like the rest of the inmates' families did. I was livid! They wanted my own family to snitch on me just for hearing my voice. We didn't talk about anything illegal, nor did we talk about anything that would compromise any type of security procedures that TDC has in place. None of the conversations even lasted that long. It was a catch-22 that the administration was trying to utilize. If my family would have snitched on me, I would not have wanted to talk to them. So, in effect, they were coming off the list anyway. My family was damned if they do, damned if they don't. I took this very personally. I wrote grievances and talked to every official I could to try to get this problem resolved.

The only solution they would give me was to tell them the officer that was bringing the phones in. I could not provide them with that information for two reasons:

1.) I am not a snitch and

2.) I did not know who was bringing them in.

I didn't get the phone I was using from an officer. I borrowed it from another inmate and there was no way I was telling them who that inmate was. When the administration saw that I had no information for them, they stopped talking to me. The grievances went unanswered, and the officials on the outside said that my family on the outside was contacted and had nothing else to say about the matter. The only thing I knew to do after that was to fight. I went on a campaign that let the administration know that I wasn't going to put up with them making my family part of their political ploy for the public. I started off with numerous uses of force. By doing this, I would let the main offices in Huntsville know that I was serious and that the matter needed to be looked into. In return, I was met with numerous forms of repressive tactics that were used to break my campaign. I was isolated on an entire section by myself with no contact with any other inmates. I was gassed excessively, time after time. I was shot with a gun; a new toy they had that resembled a paintball gun, but instead of shooting paintballs it shot balls filled with gas. They hurt when they connected! I was shot in the face and all over the body on one occasion. I didn't stop. One use of force got real messy where I was beaten down very badly by the riot team. After that, I knew that if I didn't do something serious, I was going to get hurt to the point where I would end up in the hospital. So, I started using weapons.

Weapons are not hard to come by in prison. Any thinking mind can come up with a way to make a weapon. I would take a piece of metal off the wall and sharpen it down until it came to a point. I would then find a way to brace it to the handle so it wouldn't bend when used.

The first time I tried to use a weapon it was a disaster. When I tried to swing with it the metal went flying across the cell, surprising me and the riot team. We laughed about it later knowing it was a blooper moment. After that day, I got an understanding with the officer that would be on the riot team. I told them that if they didn't want to get hurt, then they needed to refuse to come inside my cell. Most of them understood the reason why I was doing what I was doing. Some would even go to their superiors and tell them that this problem with my family needed to be resolved.

The next time I troubleshooted fairly well and cut one of the officer's pants leg, and stuck another in the kneecap. I <u>still</u> didn't get any attention for the situation. I started to get frustrated. I knew many people wouldn't agree with how I was handling the situation, but I didn't feel I had any other options. I told myself I will have one last use of force with a weapon. If it didn't draw the attention that I was looking for, then I would try a new tactic.

The reason I chose to use the weapons only during use of force was, I felt that doing it (stabbing) up close and personal to a single officer was not right in my mind. It would be as if I was blaming that officer for the situation I was going through, and that is not what I was trying to do. I rationalized that doing it through use of force was a direct shot at the administration since their riot team was their army. Their riot team was what they used to repress me. Now, if someone was hurt during that time it wouldn't be as personal, since they knew the consequences when they chose to suit up in their riot gear. The day I chose to conduct my final use of force started off horrible.

I was denied recreation because the officer was scared to deal with me. I understood them but I didn't agree with it, so I spent the day pissed off and trying to tell myself to wait until another day when I was thinking more clearly. Later that day, I had another confrontation with another officer and that made my decision for me. I blacked out my cell and refused to answer anybody that came through to check on me. By doing this, they had to suit up a riot team to open my door.

When they came, they had a few cans of gas with them. The Sergeant leading the use of force opened my food slot and emptied the first can inside my cell. They closed the slot and waited a few minutes to see if the gas would have any effect. It did not. My mind was not only focused on defeating the gas, but it was also set on making them come inside my cell. All I could think about was my family and them being punished. The Sergeant opened the door slowly and sprayed another can of gas inside the cell. He thought that since he opened the door that I would run out or move around. I didn't. I stayed right where I was inside the cell.

When he seen I wasn't falling for his tactic, he shut the door. They waited again trying to come up with another tactic to get me out of the cell. When the door opened the second time, it was no bluff. The team ran inside my cell and I had to react fast. I threw my left hand in the air, knowing they would watch my hands because of my history with weapons, and I swung low with the knife. When I swung I felt my hand stop, so I pulled back and swung again. Again, I felt my hand stop. I pulled back a third time to swing again, but my hand caught my wrist. When I felt that, I threw the knife across the room, so when I was taken to the ground I would not fall on it. I was wrestled to the ground, cuffed and shackled. When I was on the ground, the Sergeant asked the team to report any injuries.

That's when I heard, "I've been stabbed, I've been stabbed!"

The sergeant asked, "Who's been stabbed?"

"One man! Two man," the voices came back.

When I heard that, I had no feelings. This was the first time that I had ever effectively stabbed someone. I always had a gun in the streets which was a lot easier than using a knife. I remember someone telling me that it is not easy stabbing someone like it is to shoot someone. Stabbing someone is more up close, bloodier, more gruesome; unlike shooting someone, which you can do from a distance. I thought of that on numerous occasions and knew what he said was right. Could I compare it to the situation that I was in at the moment? I didn't think I could. I laid there without a smile on my face while they removed the injured men from my cell and replaced them with fresh bodies.

I was moved to a cell and left without anything but a paper gown. This gown was green and resembled one given in a hospital. This was for seven days in the winter. I slept on a cold, steel slab, freezing, but I did not complain. I knew what I did, and although I felt sorry for the officers that I stabbed, I didn't regret it at all. Days after the incident I received a visit from the Warden of the unit. He was known as a no nonsense individual. He stood about 5'6 tall and we referred to him as Napoleon. He ran death row with an iron fist, but at times with a velvet glove. He wanted to talk about the assault on the staff and why I was doing it. I broke down the entire situation to him with all of the things that showed why the punishment of my family was arbitrary. He listened attentively and agreed to most of what I was saying. He then made a deal with me. He told me if I could go one full year without assaulting any of his officers then he would personally place all of the individuals back on my list. I told him that is not a problem but that is not justice either. He agreed, but told me there was no other way that they were going to be placed back on my list since they needed the recommendation from the unit Warden first. I surrendered and told him that I would do it. We then went on to have a more intellectual conversation and learned all about each other.

Before he left my cell he asked, “Why are you on death row? I am not asking about your crime. I am asking how you ended up here. You are too smart to be here.”

I smiled because I knew that for him to admit something like that then he meant it. This guy didn’t give compliments easily.

CHAPTER 11

Sitting back inside this cell, reflecting on the first few years of my stay on death row, I try to look for the growth and the contrast in my thinking. I noticed a lot but I also noticed a bunch of the same. I began to question myself on what was holding me back from progressing myself, and knew it was that I was still looking for the same thing I searched for in the streets. I was looking for someone to love and support me.

Even before the events that involved my mom being taken off my list, we still were not seeing eye-to-eye. Since I have been on death row, I didn't get much support from her. Our relationship was the same as it was in the free world. I started to believe that it was permanently strained. After I moved out of the house and started staying with my grandma, me and my mom were better friends than we were mother and son. I think that grew out of both of us realizing that she had lost me years before and couldn't do anything about it. She knew she couldn't tell me anything. I have always wanted to repair the relationship with her, but I didn't know how. At times, I think I am more mature than she is. I understand that she is no more than 22 years older than all her kids. I understand that she was a child raising children. So, with that in mind, I continue to think maybe she is living out the years she lost as a teen and young adult now. I have tried to talk to her on an adult level but I haven't gotten through to her. We continue to bump heads to this day. Some would say we may be too much alike. Some would give the excuse that I look just like my father who she fought with daily. No matter what it is, I fear that our relationship will never be reconciled.

Being locked up in a cell 22 hours a day makes you appreciate friendships/relationships. It is so easy to be forgotten while behind these walls that the ones who do take the time out of their day to write and/or send us money to survive off of have to be appreciated. I've visited numerous people over the years from all aspects of life. I have talked to lawyers, professors, students and media people, and all of them have asked about the relationship with my mother. On numerous occasions I had to lie out of embarrassment. Who doesn't want to get along with their mother? Living inside this cell makes a man think on a very deep level. We don't have anyone to interrupt our thinking process, so once we start to think on that level, it is hard to stop without going too deep. Being on death row makes a person introspective like that. Living, in this case, is a constant battle. Only you know all of your secrets, and only you have to live with them. There are three things that will happen to a person in this situation:

One, they will lose their mind. I've witnessed this first hand. Some will ask, "Did they lose their mind, or was their mind already lost?" In some cases, I would agree to that line of thinking. Some men's minds were lost but most are just fine when they arrived. They did their best to endure the numerous situations that are placed before them. Situations from the officers to dealing with the abandonment of their families. It is always something to overcome. The mind is like a rope. It can only deal with so much stress before it snaps. Some minds can take more than others.

This makes me think of a book I read a few years ago that documented this very well. The book is called *The Lucifer Effect.* In short, it was about a study that was done at Stanford University on the *Security Housing Units* (SHU's) or "shoe," as some people like to call them. The shoe is the lockdown house that we are living in. What the study did was take a group of students and split them in half. One group was labeled "prisoners" and the other group was labeled "guards." They placed the prisoners inside mock cells and told the guards to guard them. During the time the study was going on, the guards started to mistreat the prisoners and the prisoners started to break down from the mistreatment. This study was a seven day study. Studies like this one show that the human mind is not made for isolation, mistreatment and no stimulation. Not only will it break to the point where the person cannot think rationally, but it can also make a person react in the next way.

Two, the person will become violent. A lot of men, like me, come from environments that taught us to fight against any type of repression, even if we do not fully understand. They rebel against any type of authority and authority figures. People will label them as crazy or psych patients when the problems they feel are what backed them into a corner. The *Black Panthers*, the civil rights group of the 60's, used the panther as its symbol because the panther is a feline that doesn't bother anyone, but at the same time is very dangerous. Whenever the panther feels backed into a corner and has no other options, the panther fights for its life and it fights hard. That is the same as men who react to repression.

Three, this person will excel. A lot of men come to death row and excel to where they were supposed to be in the streets. Being locked up, undistracted and drug-free can produce productive results. Some men thrive in oppressive environments. Since I have been here, I have met individuals who I didn't think needed to be on death row. I met inmates who have written books, gained degrees, raised their children and taken care of their families all from behind these walls. Even they will admit that they could not have done it if they weren't locked up in isolation. I constantly admit to myself and others that death row saved my life. As ironic as it sounds, I truly believe that death row saved my life. With the life I was living, I should not have made it to see 21.

When I did see 21 years old, I was surprised, but then I got locked up on this case two months later. I like to compare this reaction of the mind to a diamond. A diamond is considered one of the most precious jewels. It is made from the harshest of elements, carbon. Only under pressure and time can a diamond be created. I will never forget what

Reginald told me when he explained how he deals with these walls, “Keep Diamond mind, Diamond body and Diamond soul.” I try to live by that to this day.

Oppression comes in different forms here. One form is constant shakedowns (cell searches). Death row is placed on lockdown every ninety days. We are fed “Jonny sacks,” which are brown sacks consisting of one meat sandwich and a peanut butter sandwich three times a day. When our cells are searched, we are given a box three feet long and two feet high and told to fit all of our property inside. Whatever doesn’t fit has to either be sent home or thrown away. Our cells have three shelves under the bed. The shelves are four feet long, two feet high, and four feet deep. We also have two tables that have things placed on them. The rule in TDC is nothing is supposed to be on the floor and everything is to be stored on the shelves provided. When they first brought along the boxes and told us to stuff our property inside, we fought tooth and nail using their own rules against them. They didn’t relent. They were adamant on restricting our property as much as possible. It made me think: We live in a box out of a box!

CHAPTER 12

In 2011, I had a visit with a 13 year old boy. My Aunt told me he was getting into trouble at school and she wanted me to talk to him. I told her to bring him to visit me. When he came, I sat him down and asked my aunt to go sit at another table out of earshot. We began to talk. I wanted to assess his demeanor. I wanted to see if he was going to be hostile with me or if he was going to be receptive to what I was saying to him. I learned a bit of background about him.

He lived in a few different countries, being raised in a military family. He knew four different languages fluently, English, Spanish, French and Japanese. He was going to school in Sugarland, Texas, an upper class neighborhood on the outskirts of Houston. I knew what his problem was once I got the background on him. GIRLS!

I straight out asked him, "Who is she?"

He looked at me a bit bashfully and said, "What girl?"

I shook my head, knowing I hit the nail on the head, and I told him, "I was your age before and I know how it is when a fine girl is around!"

I smiled at him to let him know I understood and he could open up to me. He glanced over to my aunt and told me that the girl sat right next to him in class.

I asked him again, "Is she your girlfriend?"

He looked at me with this sad expression and said no. I asked him why, and he said a lot of guys liked her and he had not had the chance to talk to her. He wasn't a problem child. I knew he had a problem and it wasn't his behavior. It was the girl he liked. For a 13 year old, he was highly intelligent. We went on to talk about politics, current events and other issues that you wouldn't expect from a 13 year old. Then I gave him the game that I think he liked the most. I told him how to get the girl. He explained to me that the school work that is given to him was too easy. Once he was done with it he wouldn't have anything to do.

This is typical of schools with big classes today. Some kids learn at a faster rate than others, and once they are done with their work, they have to wait on the other kids to finish. Kids are still kids and I haven't met a child yet that can sit still for more than five minutes. That does not mean they are bad or have a problem. It only means that they are children. He told me when he would finish his work he would start joking around or what we call "showing out" for the girl which would cause a disturbance in class. I told him that is the reason he doesn't have the girl yet. I told him once he finishes his work, he should then go to the girl and help her with hers. He had the advantage since he finished his work first, which meant he could get to her first and they could work alone. That was his time to make his move and not get in trouble doing it. He enjoyed the idea and said he would try it out.

We continued the visit with many laughs and jokes. I let my aunt know that he wasn't a problem child and that they needed to stop treating him like one. When we treat our kids like they have a problem, they start to rebel. This creates a problem. There was too much talent and potential in him to make him feel like he was doing something wrong. After the visit I thought to myself how beneficial it could be for the community if I had the chance to talk to young people on a regular basis. This gave me the idea for my youth program: *Reaching Our Young from the Inside Out.*

I was conversing with a friend one day as we were walking in the rec yard, as we usually do in the Texas heat, waiting for the officers to come take us back to our cells. This was a good friend of mine named Tomas Gallo. I trusted his judgment since he would give it to me straight without any bullshit.

I asked him, "What do you think about a program similar to the Scared Straight program? A program in which troubled youth could come here to visit us and we can talk to them."

He smiled at me, thinking, digesting it and told me, "That might work!"

With that conversation I knew I had a good idea and that it was time to put my ideal in motion. At that time, I was still protesting. I still had a lot of anger built up in me that I was trying to ignore. I was also looked at as the leader of the protest movement. Numerous things happened that brought that into play.

October seemed to be a black month for D.R.I.V.E. In 2009, we found out that Reginald had been kicked out of the 5th Circuit Court of Appeals.

He had one avenue left for relief and knew that the chance was paper thin.

Months later, he received an execution date for October 27th 2009. I was devastated. During the time of knowing Reg we became very close. We had so much in common and came from the same neighborhoods that we connected on a higher level. We considered each other brothers and couldn't anyone tell us differently. Anyone who knew us knew if you dealt with one you had to deal with the other. Reg kept me grounded. He was the positive to my negative. When I found out he had a date, I did not know how the movement was going to survive without him. Even if he got his sentence commuted to life, he would still be gone and not be able to contribute like he did. I knew a huge void would be left in the movement.

At the time D.R.I.V.E. was having its friction. We had lost two members to life sentences (Kenneth and Gabriel). There were only four of us left here on death row. The only reason I was still affiliated with D.R.I.V.E. was Reg. I didn't get along with the other members. We didn't see eye-to-eye. There was too much power struggling going on. I was the only member that could handle everything that the administration threw at us. On numerous occasions, the other members tried to engage in use of force and get gassed, but couldn't handle the chemicals. Only Reg could handle them like I could. This caused us to bump heads on tactics. This also gave the administration a way to utilize the divide and conquer tactic that is so effective in any group that has friction with its members. During this time, I had the full respect of the administration and the other members did not like it. It made me the de facto leader in a group that agreed that there were no leaders.

As October neared, I went through the process of requesting a visit with Reg. We were housed on different pods at the time and hadn't seen each other in a few months. The request was unique because there was not any rule that made a request of that nature valid. I didn't care about any rules. I wanted to see my brother and I was going to do anything to make that happen. After a few gassings and numerous plea bargains, I did get the visit with Reg. The administration did better than I asked them for. They placed us inside a secure legal booth and left us there for eight hours on Saturday and eight hours Sunday. They knew the relationship that we had with each other, and since they had seen it was an advantage for them to let us visit (to use as leverage in the future).

When he walked in the booth I looked into his eyes. His execution date was two weeks away, and I wanted to see how he was handling the stress of being on death watch under constant scrutiny and stress. I wondered if he was putting those teachings into practice for himself. I looked at Reg and saw his eyes were shining bright like they always have. His gold frames from the designer glasses he wore were a bit dull, but that was from years of wear and tear. I looked him straight in his eyes and asked him, "How are you doing? Don't give me the long version. Give me the straight forward no bullshitting version."

Reg had a thing about long drawn out answers. I have seen some people ask him a question with him giving an answer that took almost thirty minutes to give. It was one of these psychological tactics that became part of his character.

"I'm not doing good, bruh. It is not looking good and I gotta keep the strength for the fam," he honestly told me.

Not being one of those individuals that give many verbal pats on the back such as: "it's going to be alright" or "keep your head up," I just looked at him.

When I found the words to speak I told him, "If they are going to kill, you make them work for it, bruh!"

He smiled, "I've missed you, bruh."

That broke the tension and we moved away from the elephant in the room. Those two days were great therapy for the both of us.

He left me with the words, "Bruh, don't ever give up. Keep fighting the struggle against injustice."

After the visit with Reg I came to the conclusion that it doesn't matter how much you fight against something wrong. If you don't have any power then the stance you have taken does not mean anything, no matter how right you are. On the day Reg was scheduled to be executed I had my attorney come visit me. I wanted to be in the visitation room with him until he left the visit. That morning showed me that the day was not going to be normal. The officers came around to set up recreation like they normally do, but when they came to my door they told me that they will set me up for the dayroom later. I knew then that the administration had put me on a security lockdown. They do this on special occasions when they feel that someone will try to slow down a process that is supposed to run smoothly. They were right about me because if I had seen my brother protest his murder, I was protesting his murder.

I knew I had an attorney visit coming, so I figured that they could not leave me on security lockdown for long. They couldn't deny the attorney's visit. I waited and waited for the escort team to come take me to visit. When I saw noon time approaching I knew something had to be up. At noon, the administration will cease all movement to get the offender off the unit. After noon time, I was pissed! I knew I wasn't there for my brother as the support and backbone the way I wanted to be. I sat in my cell wondering what he would think about not seeing me out there like I promised him. I felt like I let him down on what may be his final day to live. When I was finally escorted to the visitation room it was quiet and all of the commotion that surrounds the process of getting the inmate with the date off the unit had died down. It was the aura of silence there that envelopes the visitation room as those visiting see the process for themselves. It's the same process that they fear they may have to deal with one day. Later that day, I was in the dayroom waiting on any kind of news that came through the radio telling me that my brother was coming back.

I had three different people listening to three different stations. I didn't want to miss a thing. At 6:00 p.m. we still didn't hear anything on the radio that indicated if he was getting a stay of execution. I paced the dayroom, nervously hoping the worst didn't happen to my brother, and that our news sources were just slow in reporting the good news. At 6:09 p.m., I started crying. I didn't even think that it was over yet, but my body knew that he was gone. I felt him die. A piece of me went with him that day.

CHAPTER 13

Reaching Our Young is still in the infant stages, but I am working hard to get it off the ground. The idea went from a thought to a full fledged movement. When I was coming up in the system, I was sent through the *Scared Straight program*. What they did was send troubled youth to the nearest prison. When we arrived there, we were stripped naked and given “prison garb,” which consisted of oversized pants and an oversized shirt. We were then sent through a few of the routines that the regular prisoners had to go through, but a bit more aggregated than usual. First we were given an “Aggie” which is a work tool that resembles a hoe with a spike on the opposite side. It is used to work the soil in the fields to plant crops. The prisons in Texas looked exactly like the old slave plantations from 1700’s and 1800’s. They are run the same too. The structure resembles the same hierarchy. The warden and his assistant warden are the same as the “Master of the Plantation”. Everyone else (Major, Captain, Lieutenant, and Sergeant) were the overseers.

As we were working in the fields, they had a couple of officers riding horses with long shotguns in a holster and a pistol strapped to their sides. I saw them spitting chewing tobacco and using the word “boi” like it was his favorite word out of the dictionary. None of this resonated with me until I came to prison and saw the way things are from African American history. Once we finished in the fields we were taken to the administration segregation (Ad Seg) of the unit where the "worst of the worst" inmates of the unit were housed.

They placed us in an isolation cell for an hour and fed us lunch which consisted of what TDC likes to call a "food loaf." A food loaf is a punishment meal that has all of the food from the current meal that is being served, blended together into a bread mixture and baked until it comes together. It sort of looks like a hot pocket, and smells bad! They fed it to us to show what we would be eating if we didn't follow the rules in prison.

They let us out of the cells after an hour, and pranced us down the walkway in front of the offenders who began to hoot, holler, and whistle at us. The offenders would tell us how they were going to "fuck" us and "cum" in our mouths, etc.

After that, they took us to a room to meet some inmates. Once settled in, twelve inmates came running in the room yelling at the top of their lungs. These inmates were supposed to scare us. The only problem with that was I looked at them and instantly knew four or five of them from the hood. Once they "calmed down" from all of that noise, we were broken off into groups for counseling. I was taken to the side by the individual that I knew and asked to give an update on what was going on in the streets. I was asked to send messages back to old girlfriends and asked to contact family that had forgotten these individuals.

When I left the prison I knew I wanted to come back. There was nothing that I seen that deterred me from wanting or caring about going to prison. In the neighborhood that I grew up in and numerous others across America, it is a badge to wear to go to the penitentiary. By going, you have the distinction of saying that you survived the concrete jungle, prison. I know that *Reaching Our Young* can change that mindset. I know if one of those individuals would have sat me down and taken the time to talk to me, and not worry about getting messages out to the public, it would have made a difference in the way I thought about prison.

What I am going to do is make sure I find at least one kid that is traveling down the path to prison and help change his or her life. Anybody who thinks that an inmate on death row does not have a purpose in life anymore does not know that life does not end just because someone says you cannot change yourself and be an asset to society. I will show them not by my word, but by sending them a kid that is on his or her way to college because I showed them that prison is not the place to be.

I WILL SUCCEED! I've learned from M.E.; From My Experiences!

Christopher Young

CHAPTER 14
(LAST RIDE - LAST WORDS)

Who wants to think what their last words are going to be? Could you imagine what it would feel like sitting in a cell fifteen feet away from the room where you're supposed to be murdered? As time ticks away, what would be going through your head? I don't know how a normal human being can stay sane while knowing the time that they're supposed to be murdered?

It all starts off with a four hour visit with my loved ones. Many people handle this last visit differently, some laugh and enjoy while others cry and can't control themselves. I guarantee it will be the fastest four hours of my life. This visit starts at 8:00 a.m. and goes until 12:00 p.m. on the day of my murder. Around 11:55 a.m., a six-man riot team approaches my visiting cage, fully equipped with crowd control gas, led by the warden waiting to escort me to my last ride.

The warden asks, "Are you ready?"

Now with everything that's going through my head, how in the hell am I supposed to answer a question like that? What if I tell him no? Will he let me stay? So, now they cuff me up for well over the 1000th time, and lead me down a long walkway to a van that will transport me to my final cage. Before I enter the van, I am shackled with about fifteen extra pounds of chains from waist to ankles. I, then, am strapped in the van and we're on our way to the Walls Unit – where Texas murders men and women an average of twenty times a year. As myself and five other guards, including the warden from the unit I'm being transported to, ride down the country roads, I enjoy the scenery as it flies by. I know this can be the last time I see nature, so I take in the clouds and pastures the best I can.

We arrive at the *Walls Unit* that's right in the middle of the city of Huntsville, Texas. I see protestors that oppose, and spectators that support my murder. The guards lead me inside the prison toward my small five foot by nine foot cage, and unshackle me to let me loose like the animal they've been trying to breed over the years.

I sit on the bunk with a million thoughts going through my head, as a pastor walks up to the bars and asks, "Do you want to accept Christ in your life?"

I sit there and stare at him for a second, and shake my head, not because I don't want to accept Christ, but the man didn't even ask me my religion, let alone have I already accepted Him!

I tell the pastor, "I'm okay. We have a great relationship."

I sit there with nothing to do for about three hours. The guards come to escort me to prepare for my final meal. I stare at the state-issued food that they have to offer. It's not what I asked for! I wanted some of Mama's homemade chitterlings, hog maws, cornbread, collard greens, and fresh peach cobbler. But instead, I'm looking at the same old pork chop and what they would call greens, but I call spinach. I didn't eat the porkchop the whole time I've been incarcerated. I decline the meal and ask to be put back in my cage. It's not going to digest anyways! I'm led back to my cage and a state-issued radio is there awaiting me. I don't want to listen to music, so I try to catch the news and hear something about the final rulings on my case.

Then, the guards ask if I want to make a five minute phone call. A five minute phone call! Hell, it would take five minutes just to connect with who I'm calling. So again, I decline the so-called friendly treatment. The warden then comes to my door with what he called *The Riot Act*. *The Riot Act* is the procedure that the prison officials have to go through to make sure I get to the execution chamber. It says any force necessary can be used to ensure the process is carried out.

Before I let him start reading, I interrupt him to ask, "Do I look like I can start a damn riot? You're the one with the riot team! I should be reading you the riot act!"

He continues on with his procedure. I pay him no mind since its almost 5:30 p.m. and my murder is supposed to take place at 6:00 p.m.!

A million thoughts flow through my head and it's hard to just focus on one, so I think of my daughter. I haven't seen her in over five hours, and her beautiful smile is seared in my brain. This brings a much needed smile to my face, as my mind switches thoughts. How will my mother break the news to her of how her daddy died? How will she react? This wipes the smile completely off my face and hurts me worse than thinking about my murder thats about to take place. I’m snapped back into reality by marching footsteps and a riot team standing in front of my cage. The warden says it's time. I just look at him because the words came out of his mouth with such ease. I get the feeling he wants to do this. I’m handcuffed and taken to a room where I’m fitted with an anal plug and penial catheter or an adult sized diaper· This is to make sure my bowels don’t make a mess. Don’t want spectators to see feces everywhere while the life is sucked out of me!

I’m then placed on a stretcher because I will not walk to my own murder, and rolled toward the chamber. This is the longest ride of my life, and I notice the last. I’m transported to the gurney and strapped down at my ankles, waist and chest. My arms are spread out to make me look like a cross and strapped at my wrist and upper arm. The needles are then inserted into place. Once everything is set for the murder, the warden signals for the curtains to be drawn. I now see the victim’s family on one side standing with the district attorney that convicted me. He’s smiling! I can’t believe he’s smiling! I turn my head to the other side of the room and notice my family crying. The warden then says the speech that I can tell has been recited over a hundred times.

“Christopher Young #999508, you are about to be executed by the State of Texas. Do you have any last words?”

Once I begin to speak, I start to taste a salty fluid in my throat, and notice no words are coming out my mouth! It feels like I can't breathe, that I'm suffocating. I can't tell anybody because I can't talk. Everything is going blurry. I notice my mother waiting on me to at least say I love you, but I can't talk!

Everything goes black.

EPILOGUE

by Stefan Heikens

Chris Young was executed by lethal injection on Tuesday, July 17, 2018 in Huntsville, Texas. Just the day before, there had been a meeting with Mitesh Patel, the son of the murder victim, where Chris and Mr. Patel talked in person for the first time. They had never met before. Mr. Patel had seen video footage of Chris and decided he wanted to meet Chris himself, especially because Chris had made it clear in the video how much he would like to apologize in person. This footage, and especially the visit to Chris himself, convinced Mr. Patel how wrong the death penalty would be in this case. Thus, Mr. Patel tried to secure a pardon for Chris. In Mr. Patel's opinion, Chris simply deserved a second chance because he had long since ceased to be the person he had been at the time of the crime. Even Chris' lawyers cited his growth in prison: they claimed he prevented both an inmate's assault on a guard, as well as a suicide, and that he eased racial tensions on death row. But all appeals had been rejected by the Texas Board of Pardons and Paroles; the reasoning for this decision is unknown to the public, and individual members usually cast their votes remotely without comment or a hearing.

Chris had been slowly preparing for his own death. In the last days before his execution date, he convinced his family to stay away from the execution. He also talked to his friends on death row about his impending death. He asked them to take extra good care of his Aunt Valerie, and at the same time asked her to take care of those same friends. Thus, even in his last days, he forged a bond between these people without them knowing it; a bond that would endure long after his death.

Chris spoke to Mr. Patel about his attempts to reach young, impressionable youth while still in the cell, to warn them of the dangers that had brought him to this place, and also about how much he regretted what he had done. It was a long, intense and, above all, extraordinary conversation that probably most people could not understand. Mr. Patel was able to see that the once 21-year-old boy who was drunk and angry when he unintentionally shot Mr. Patel's father had grown into a man. After the visit, he said, "*It's really unfortunate that the board didn't hear our request for clemency. I feel sadness for his family. They're going to be walking down the same path my family has been on the last fourteen years ... Two wrongs don't make a right, killing Chris doesn't change my path, my history. It only affects a whole other set of people...*"

The next day, everything had to happen very quickly. At 5:45 a.m. Chris was taken to the shower, where he could clean himself one last time. A half an hour later, he was already lying on his cot again, and slept for the last time. At 7:55 a.m., he was taken to the visiting room where he had to wait in a cage for his aunt who would be seated on the other side of the bulletproof glass. Aunt Valerie, the woman he had chosen to be his spiritual advisor, was then able to speak to him at 8:25 a.m. and as the first visitor that day. The prisoner is allowed to select a spiritual advisor to accompany him to the door of the execution chamber, and Chris preferred to have someone familiar with him rather than the prison chaplain.

But since each visit was only allowed to last two hours, there were several visits that day for Chris who had been allowed to sit in the visiting room longer than was customary. Valerie and Chris laughed, cried and prayed together. Chris asked his aunt one last time to not watch his execution. He wished that she would accompany him as far as she could, but without burdening her with the sight of his death. Valerie, who would see Chris again later, gave up her last hour visit to a friend of Chris's who also wanted to say goodbye. It was difficult to get everything that needed to be done on this last day. Who can count the hours until they die? Who among us would know how to prioritize?

So, they took turns as time passed. In the adjacent cages, other death row inmates sat saying goodbye to Chris. Again and again, they called over to him and he answered, encouraging them. As usual on days like this, as many inmates as possible had scheduled their once-a-week visit on this day so they could send Chris a final message.

Probably the hardest visit was yet to come for Chris, as at 10 a.m. Chris sat across from his mother and stepfather. The three had two hours to say goodbye to each other, then they would never see each other again in this life. At 11:25 a.m., the last photos were taken in which Chris could be seen alive, shortly after which his mother also had to leave him. Afterwards, Chris was taken directly to the *Texas state penitentiary* in Huntsville, the prison where he would die. There in the death watch he met Valerie again, and spent some time with her there, separated by black wire mesh. In the room outside the death chamber, he was already waiting for her. He asked her to take a good look at the room and remember everything. Valerie saw the phone from which he would once again call his family. Back at home, many of his family members were waiting for a call. Valerie also saw the door through which he would be brought to his death. She would never forget the number 17 that was written above it because this was the last door he would ever walk through on his own two feet.

Chris and Valerie were both able to slide their fingers through the wire, but their fingers still did not touch. For twelve long years, Chris had not been touched lovingly by anyone, and even now they would not allow him to. But Chris and Valerie were able to talk and make plans for a future Chris would not live to see. Chris talked about what else he had planned for his life, how he had wanted to help others, and how he would now have to give that task to others.

"I'm not ready to die. I'm not finished!" he said.

He cried, remembering all the people he loved, and Valerie comforted him as best she could. It is a human need to be touched, to be held, but even that was denied Chris until the end. At least in spirit he should be free and know that he was loved. Valerie told him that she did not think clemency was good enough and that she had asked God to set him free. She told him that maybe she should have been more specific in her prayer because this day would be the day that he would never have to go back to prison. She told him that the state could have his body, but they could never have his spirit or his vision. Unless a seed falls to the ground and dies, it can bear no fruit. She promised him to never let his vision die, and that it's okay for him to go and chill out with his dad who was murdered back when Chris was 8 years old.

She also shared the story of when Sondra, Chris' cousin, and her dad went fishing. Chris had always wanted to go fishing. Sondra was barely learning how to fish. But when they returned home, her ice chest had a number of nice sized fish. Her dad, however, only caught a couple of small fish. When Valerie saw it, she told them that Sondra brought home the meal and her dad brought home the snack. Chris laughed and laughed! He always loved Valerie's sense of humor. He then told Valerie that she had to go.

Her response was, "It's not time yet", but he answered that he still had work to do.

He was writing a letter to Cornel West and he wanted to finish it before he would talk to his family for the last time. He bowed his head as Valerie prayed for him. It would be the last time he would see her face or hear her voice.

As Valerie was leaving she told one of the guards, "You are killing a good man today," and then she heard him laughing with the other guards. She said to the guard, "Who does that when someone is about to be executed?"

A few minutes before his death, those same guards came to Chris and took him to the execution chamber. It was 6:03 p.m.! There, he was strapped to a cot with his arms spread out before an electrocardiogram was attached to him. He was covered with a white sheet. After he was restrained, two intravenous tubes were inserted, one tube in each arm. The tubes were threaded through an opening in the wall that leads to the anteroom where the executioner was located.

Then, the curtain was pulled back to the visitor's room. There, they all should have been sitting: the victim's family, Chris' own family, but no one had come. They had all respected Chris' wish to die alone. From outside, you could hear the noise of the demonstrators who came to protest the death penalty at every execution. As they did so, they passed a megaphone to anyone who wanted to say anything else to the death row inmate from outside.

Chris was asked if he had anything else to say and hc rcplied, "I want to make sure the Patel family knows I love them like they love me. Make sure the kids in the world know I'm being executed, and that those kids I've been mentoring keep this fight going. I'm good, Warden."

Then, the poison compounded pentobarbital was introduced into his body at 6:13 p.m. This puts the inmate into a deep sleep and can reach effective clinical concentrations in the brain within thirty seconds.

After receiving the anesthetic, Chris started grunting and said, "I taste it in my throat" before he passed away.

After Chris was officially pronounced dead at 6:38 p.m., he was transported out of the room. The official witnesses signed that the execution had taken place and were led out of the building by the guards. Chris, on the other hand, was taken to another room where Valerie was allowed to see him one more time. She had been the last to speak to him when he was alive and was now the first to see him dead. His face was peaceful, and she was allowed fifteen minutes with him before he was placed in a body bag and taken away from her. During that short time, she kissed him, talked to him, and touched him for the first time in years. Chris, who had spent the last twelve years in solitary confinement, only to end up being punished for a crime he had always regretted, finally had his freedom back. He was buried on July 23, 2018 next to his father. This book is part of his legacy.

FEBRUARY 17, 2019

by Valerie Harris

It was seven months ago today since I last saw him

Seven months since I heard his voice

Heard his laugh, heard him cry

It was seven months ago today since

I ran my hands across his head

Placed my hand upon his heart

Saw a single tear in the corner of his right eye

It's been seven months ago today when I kissed his face

Felt his sweat as he laid still upon a gurney at the front of the church called "Grace"

A guard, a mortician and a church lady stood by watching me, staring quietly

To ensure I would not pull back the sheets to see his wounds

To witness how he died at the hands of Justice

It's been seven months and there is still a hole in my heart

Because Justice stood in the face of Grace and said "No Mercy"

Perhaps I should feel joy

Knowing that he's been set free

No more chains can bind him

Death can no longer hold him hostage

Because he is alive in me and alive in those who love him

It's been seven months ago today since life and death embraced one another

And you crossed over to the other side of life

It's been seven months ago today when you Jasiri – my fearless warrior

Laid down your sword and I picked it up to fight for a righteous cause

Driven now to do something greater than myself

Joining forces with others to rescue our young from the fate of merciless death

Finding those who are lost in the web of uncertainty

Impacting lives with new hope, new vision, new direction and second chances

And I realize how truly blessed I am knowing that I am not alone

You left me with others who will fight with me and for me

Who will stand for true Justice

I recognize that I am just a small piece of the Masterpiece designed by Our Creator
You were a piece of that fabric that has now been placed among the lights of heaven

My joy will come when the Master's work is complete in me

When I take my place among the stars

But until then, I will lift up the banner and carry the flaming sword

As we fight for the cause of justice for our children and future generations

Seven months ago today I said goodbye

But only for a little while, until my day is done

CHRISTOPHER YOUNG

by Perry E. Williams

In the eyes of the public,
Christopher Young is a heathen.
A degenerate. A heartless killer.
Someone who can't be rehabilitated.

Yet, in my eyes, he's the cream
of the crop, a god amongst men,
and a diamond in the rough to name a few.

He's my brother, one who I've strived
to be like, yet pushes me to be better
than he is, and to reach my full potential.

And, if it wasn't for him, I wouldn't be
here today, after two failed attempts on
my life at my own hands.

Because he helped me see and believe
in what I didn't believe or see in myself.

So, in closing, Christopher Young
is a giver of knowledge, wisdom
and understanding, and someone who
I wouldn't be the man I am today if
I wasn't blessed with meeting him.

This poem is from the book
OPEN EYES by **PERRY E. WILLIAMS**

CHRISTOPHER A. YOUNG

09/24/1983 – 07/17/2018

GONE, BUT NOT FORGOTTEN